Insightful Comments about this Book

"A great marketing guide for small business management."
Peter Bretchger- President Integrated Marketing Works

"A much-needed addition to the discipline of Marketing. It takes us to the heart of the matter of why business can't succeed without it."
Peter Johns – President Johns Design Group

"An excellent primer for any business manager or owner who must be reminded that business is all about marketing."
Jason Orr – President Optimal Performance Group

"Now I can show all my clients why they must do Marketing."

Paul Myles, President Myles Researches

This is the first time I have really understood why marketing can work in my company. I highly recommend it to all business leaders who want to grow to the next level."

Peter E. Sulman, Past Partner McCarthy Robinson Engineering Inc.

"A fascinating, interesting, and insightful story that brilliantly examines the basic concept of marketing as a business technique of value."

Graham Denton, President of Product Initiatives

Accelerate Marketing Growth

A Modern Business Parable at CONE Inc.

A journey of business discovery using marketing to move your company and its products and services to the next level of volume, revenue, and profit.

R. Stephen Rayfield

Second Edition

ESIL Publishing, Oshawa, Ontario, Canada

Accelerated Marketing Growth
A Modern Business Parable at CONE Inc.

By Stephen Rayfield

Published by:

ESIL Publishing,
638 Buchan Avenue, Oshawa, Ontario, Canada L1J 3A3
www.stephenrayfield.com

Rayfield, R. Stephen
Accelerate Marketing Growth
A Modern Business Parable at CONE Inc.
R. Stephen Rayfield
1. Marketing - Management. 2. Business - Marketing.
3. Small business - Management.

Includes bibliographical references and index

ISBN: eBook 978-1-990704-04-8
ISBN: Paperback 978-1-990704-05-5

First Edition Printing 2024

Acknowledgments

My sincere thanks to:

Dr. Al Coke, who unlocked the juggernaut of how to set out this message and then provided sound advice on the story; Graham Denton, for his reassuring comments and skillful handling of improvements; and Paul Myles, who, having been there, provided assurance that the story was worthwhile publishing.

Additional thanks to those who inspire.

Peter Johns has inspired me to continue to seek the "*Why*" of marketing.

Elizabeth Rayfield gave the right level of faith to this project and then drafted the original manuscript.

Many seminar participants and clients helped hone the ideas and continued to support the book's central theme. You must understand the opportunity to accelerate marketing growth and build into all your marketing efforts. This alone will add to your company and products. It will take you to the next level of volume, revenue and profits.

Pine Cone of Clarity™

This represents points of clarity in the copy, illustrations, models or formulas for you to use to improve your integrated marketing efforts as you begin your own journey of discovery.

About the Author Stephen Rayfield

R. Stephen Rayfield is a Marketing Strategy Mentor and President/ Founder of ESIL, an interim marketing firm, which educates, creates and manages key business marketing programs and integrated brand marketing system processes.

Living in southern Ontario, he has traveled internationally on training, speaking assignments and mentoring.

His unique business background includes working for Fortune 100 companies such as General Mills, Ralston Purina and Hiram Walker as well as ISI Systems and AdvancePCS. He has gained extensive hands-on experience in such business areas as Marketing Coaching, Strategic Planning Cycles, Marketing Planning and New Product or Service Systems Development.

Stephen is a Marketing Strategy Mentor and authour. He was a course leader for several AMA/ ESIL marketing seminars including: "Successful Product Manager," "Fundamentals of Marketing" and "Advance Course in Strategic Marketing" and is a speaker in other Marketing Programs.

As an instructor at the University of Toronto School of Continuing Studies, he developed and taught marketing innovation.

His latest major project is writing this second business book, which he began after many people throughout North America asked him to ***"Help me tell my boss why we need marketing."***

FORWARD

There are many books that describe how to market your company. This is not one of those books. Instead, this work proves a case for why marketing is a critical element for managing a successful business. It helps you to understand the real value of marketing for your company, regardless of whether it is big or small, new or established, private or public.

Many people think they are correctly marketing their capabilities and abilities, but they are not. They do not really understand this thing called 'Marketing' and what value it holds for all shareholders.

This book describes a mythical company called CONE Inc. and its need to grow. The president becomes aware that the missing link in his business formula is the absence of a strong integrated marketing plan. With this realization, he sets out on a journey to find the critical information.

The president is joined on his journey of discovery by a senior staff member. Together they explore and are guided through the marketing process by a third person with the wisdom of business and actual marketing experience. With their guide, they explore, chapter by chapter, the key elements of the critical area of marketing.

Enjoy your read of this interesting business parable. It provides you with understandings of the key role that marketing plays in complex but fundamental business techniques. The sound learning and specific formulas in each chapter will help you to make integrated marketing work for you and your business.

Dr. Alfred Coke, Ph.D.
Al Coke & Associates, International

1

As he opened his office door, Adam glanced at the nameplate: Adam Jeffrey, President, CONE Inc.

“I’ve really got a key business-building stumbling block,” he said aloud as he took his seat behind his cluttered desk, “I just cannot put my finger on it.” When the door opened, he was reaching for the phone, and Sarah Pounder, CONE’s CFO, walked into his office.

“Adam, did you get a chance over the weekend to think about the third-quarter revenue figures and year-end revenue and profit projections I gave you Friday afternoon?" asked Sarah. "Yes, I did Sarah, and it confirms what we talked about last week. We've got a major growth issue, and I just don't know how to address it."

"Well then," Sarah said in her usual matter-of-fact way, "let's talk about it some more and see if we can clarify the issue."

"We're just not growing fast enough, and I don't know why!" Adam said, exasperated. "That's the real issue."

"Okay," Sarah said calmly. So, what are the plusses and minuses?"

Adam took a breath. "Right, let's get some coffee for you and some tea for me, and we'll talk as much as it takes. This is important and we must get to the bottom of it. I've got to get a handle on this issue if I'm going to lead the company to the next level of development in terms of volume and profits."

As they walked to the kitchen, Sarah mentally reviewed what had sparked this issue. The third quarter sales and revenue figures had shown that they were growing but only by 2.1%, barely matching the industry growth rate of 2.3%.

John Evergreen, one of the more vocal members of the board of directors, recently mentioned over lunch that they were hoping CONE Inc. could grow to the next level of business revenues. If CONE management could just get moving toward solid low double-digit sales growth after virtually flat performance for several years, the board would support investing in business structure.

They also needed to generate a specific ROI the Board had set.

Sarah had been with CONE Inc. from day one, starting in accounts payable. An organized person with a solid sense of business she had grown with the company, and when CONE reached the point where it needed a CFO,

Sarah had the experience and the credentials to fit the position.

Adam had started as head of sales with a solid background in several industries and an excellent head for business. He had finished an executive MBA program and moved into the president's position a little over a year ago. His instinctive feeling for the business and his willingness to listen to suggestions had added to his career movement and his company's support.

Sarah and Adam sat down at the round table in his office and looked out the window at the large pine trees behind CONE Inc.'s headquarters just to gather their thoughts.

They both knew this was a key meeting and that it was crucial to resolve this business-building issue.

Adam got up, moved to the whiteboard, and began. "If we look around us, we can say:

Cone Inc Today

1. We have moved from one product to many products.
2. We have a solid management team that works well together.
3. The sales team is working hard, and we can see they are really trying.
4. Our products are a mix of different share levels in their various markets, and we know they are of really great quality.
5. The people in the company certainly seem motivated.
6. Our client list is growing.
7. Our distribution and client coverage are solid.

"Alright," said Sarah. "We seem to have all the business structure and elements to grow. Why isn't it happening?" Adam contemplated the seven points he had made on the flipchart. "We've also done a good job of reviewing where we are in terms of competitive products in the market."

They were both silent as they stared at the list on the flipchart. It wasn't getting any more straightforward. They could not see what prevented them from moving to the next level. At last, Adam had an idea and broke the silence with a thought.

"Sarah, we need someone to help us see the picture differently."

Sarah thought for a minute. "Adam, that new neighbour of mine is a nice guy with lots of business experience," said Sarah. "He's teaching business and marketing at the university this fall."

"He said if I ever need help, he'd gladly give it. Phillip and I helped his family when they moved in, and we've helped them find their way around the city. Why don't I talk to him tonight and see if he can help us get some insight into this?"

"Tell me more about him," asked Adam with some interest.

"Well, he has a business background in several different industries and has worked in industrial and consumer markets. He recently decided to change careers rather than retire. He's been a lifelong learner, and he felt he could help students get started with his real-world experience and *all that book stuff* as he calls it. He feels strongly about giving back some of the ideas, concepts, and practical things he has learned in his career.

"This guy talks about results and how to get them in the real world, not just theory and academic business models," Sarah was excited now. "Adam, an hour with him could be very worthwhile."

Adam trusted Sarah's business judgment. For a finance person, she had a good grasp of key business options and reality, not just numbers. It was becoming clear that despite all their experience they were not finding the answers.

The next day, Adam read Sarah's email saying her neighbour, Peter McPhadden, would be glad to meet with them. He had suggested that since the university was midway between his home and their office, he could meet from 10:30 to 11:30 a.m. Wednesday in his university office in the Rayfield Building.

Adam checked his schedule on his iPhone and noted another meeting just before that time. But his instincts told him this issue was a priority, so he rescheduled the other meeting and confirmed 10:30 a.m. Wednesday with Peter McPhadden and Sarah.

"What do I want from this meeting?" he asked himself. One hour was not long. But it would be long enough to meet the man, get some of his background, an idea of his abilities, and just get a sense of whether he could help.

2

Adam and Sarah were surprised that Peter's office looked much like theirs. It was not what they had expected from a university professor. There are no piles of dusty books or files on the floor. Peter rose to meet them, and they were even more surprised to see he was dressed like a Fortune 500 company president in a blue suit, white shirt, and red-striped Brooks Brothers tie.

"Welcome to my office". Peter said warmly, offering his hand.

Adam thought to himself, *'This guy's a little formal. I hope this is going to work.'*

They shook hands all around, and Peter invited them to sit down and get comfortable. "I have coffee or tea," he said. Let's just talk a little and see if I can help you."

After having a hot cup of tea, Adam started the conversation by saying, "We have a business issue, or maybe two or three, that we need some help with. But first, I would like to understand a little bit about your business background."

Peter said, "Yes. I started in sales straight from university, and after a couple of years, I ran a small sales group in one of the divisions of my company. We sold industrial products, and I enjoyed it. But when an opportunity came up to move into marketing, I'd always been interested in that area so I went for it. That's when I really found that I enjoyed business. It was like I could wrap my arms around all the components that make products happen."

"After a few years, I moved to a packaged goods company that produced candies. The division I joined made boxed chocolates, like those you get at Christmas, Easter, or Mother's Day, and some regular candies. It was very different from industrial products, but it helped me to focus on a different way of marketing and to understand the solid basics better. We had all the same business techniques as my previous job, like advertising, trade shows, pricing, but now they were focused on consumers."

Peter continued. "From there, I became vice president of marketing at a different kind of company, a not-for-profit one. We developed programs, secured merchandise for schools, and helped them sell the items to make money. You know when school kids come around selling light bulbs, garden tools or chocolate bars, things like that?"

"It was an interesting company, and I helped it to grow by using marketing tools, models, and techniques. We tripled sales and increased the profitable revenue in my seven years there."

He sighed and sipped his tea. "Then I reached that golden time when retirement was coming closer, and I decided to move to this town. My wife and I have always liked the area, and there was the opportunity to teach at the university. I have a lot of business background, and I thought I could combine that with some real-world learning, marketing models and templates, and other book stuff to give the students a good start."

"When I was at college, my mentor was a businessman who taught part-time and ran his successful manufacturing business. That fellow always gave me different insights, not just the straight academic models."

He paused and then said, "So, that's my business background. Having heard all that, am I still of interest to you?" He said it with a little smile.

Adam looked at Sarah and said, "Well, it all sounds fine to me. Let's discuss our business situation, and then you can decide if *we* interest you."

"Excellent," Peter said, his smile warmer now. "Please tell me a little about yourself and your company, Adam."

For the next fifteen minutes, Adam and Sarah talked about their business backgrounds and CONE Inc. They covered in some detail the seven key items Adam had noted on the whiteboard during their meeting in Adam's office. After noting each item, they discussed what they had uncovered in their analyses.

CONE Inc. was an interesting company that had grown from two smaller companies into one larger one. It was clear to Peter that it had now grown to a point where they needed serious business help to grow to the subsequent sales revenue and profit level.

"Well, Adam, I think one of the big issues is that your company has grown to the point where you need that all-important business discipline called Marketing."

Adam stated, "I believe all of us do marketing now. We talk to the customers and we have trade show stuff. We do brochures and we do some advertising. Last year we had a PR campaign for a new item we launched."

Peter nodded. "I understand. But you really need to think of marketing as a set of business methodologies. Many tools in the marketing area can be used to help business grow. First, we have to really understand what marketing is," Peter said matter-of-factly, emphasizing the word marketing.

"Let me give you some things to think about in this area, and then maybe we can meet again tomorrow or the next day to flesh it out. How would that be, Adam?"

Adam sounded unconvinced. "I'm not sure about this marketing thing just yet, Peter. I don't understand why it is so important."

"Okay," Peter said. "We'll start easy. We've identified all the things that are working in the company or that we think are working in the company, right?"

"Right," Adam said with conviction.

"I think we've done a pretty solid review of CONE Inc.," added Sarah. "We know we're doing a lot of good things. But they're not working as strongly for us as we expected."

"That's right," Peter said. "Now you need to apply what marketing provides as a business tool, which is a focus. Marketing does many things. It allows you to focus on products, understand customer needs, and recognize when to get rid of products. With the right tools, you can provide accelerated marketing growth for your business."

"But aren't we all doing marketing now?" Adam said, looking quickly at Sarah.

Sarah replied, "Well, I thought so, but now I'm not so sure. We've never really defined marketing at CONE Inc."

Peter then suggested, "Let's start by doing a short survey I used to use at The Candy Company. Whenever we bought a new company, we used this survey to find out what the folks at that company thought marketing was and how they were doing it. An outside marketing company created the survey, and we found it a very effective tool. It helped us understand what level of marketing the new company was at and helped us identify the next development steps for the new group."

He sipped his tea and sat back. "You have to be careful not to try things that are too sophisticated or too academic when what is really needed is the simple thing."

"The simple thing?" Sarah asked hopefully.

"Remember Henry Ford," Peter said. "He said you can buy any car you want as long as it's a Model T and any color as long as it's black. That was simple, straightforward, and focused. Let's not get hung up on multiple colors and multiple models if all we really need is a Model T." Peter put his empty cup down with a clink. "In understanding a business issue, using the fundamental techniques is important. We don't want to use complex models when we really need primary models."

Peter stood up. "I'm going to give you this survey to fill out. When you are ready to talk about it, give me a call, and we will set a time."

Adam hesitated, then said, "Okay, we will do the survey. Let's set a time for next Monday."

Peter got up and emailed each of them a copy of the Marketing Effectiveness Survey (1) from the computer on his desk.

"It's important that you each do the survey separately to give a broader perspective of what is being done now at CONE Inc.," said Peter. "I find the survey most effective when several people in a company do it. You'll be surprised how close you both are in your individual scoring!"

Adam reviewed the six question sheets and commented, "This won't take long. Maybe we can meet by Friday?" Peter looked at his schedule and confirmed he could make it at 1:30 p.m. on Friday. Adam replied that was fine, as long as they met at his office since he had several Friday meetings scheduled later in the day. Sarah was fine with the meeting at CONE Inc., and the time worked for her.

On the way back, Adam mulled things over with Sarah. "I'm not sure yet if this is the right thing. We need to dig a little deeper at the next meeting."

Sarah agreed. "Let's do the survey questions first. Then we'll decide how we feel and what we want to do."

When Adam returned to his office, he opened the marketing survey on his laptop. After a brief overview of the questions, he thought, "I'll do this tonight at home, when I can really think about it," and tucked it into his take-home briefcase.

3

That night, Adam sat in his den with another cup of hot tea and the survey in front of him. He devoted 45 minutes to carefully considering his answers to the Marketing Effectiveness Survey© (Note: Send an email to Stephen for the complete survey). The questions covered a variety of business areas.

As he read through it, he recalled what Peter had said when he handed him the survey. The Marketing Effectiveness Questionnaire is intended to do three things:

1. Identify how you are currently approaching the marketing function.
2. Review in an overview fashion how other departments are integrating with the marketing group.
3. Identify areas that you can take action on to improve the marketing effort immediately.

The first question clearly set the tone for the survey:

1. Does management recognize the importance of designing
the company to serve the needs and wants of chosen markets?

- Management primarily thinks in terms of selling current and new products to whoever will buy them. ____ 0

- Management thinks in terms of serving a wide range of markets and needs with equal effectiveness. ____1

- Management thinks in terms of serving the needs and wants of well-defined markets chosen for their long-run growth and profit potential for the company. ____ 2

"Each has a rating and needs to have an answer," Adam read from the pages. "And I have to answer 0 or 1 or 2 as a rating for each question. Hmmm. OK I can do this."

By the time he got to question 4, Adam was not feeling quite so good about CONE Inc. His answers gave him some key information about where the company was in its lifecycle of business development and marketing, in particular.

He wondered how Sarah was doing with her survey and what kind of rating she was giving. Peter had said they would have similar answers but had doubts as he worked through the survey.

He did like the way the survey was structured. It gave him some options to really consider when thinking about his company. While more work than he expected, he was glad to invest the time to complete the survey.

He looked at question 4.

4. Is there high-level marketing integration and control of the major marketing functions?

- No. Sales and other marketing functions are not integrated at the top and there is some unproductive conflict.

  ____ 0

- Somewhat. There is formal integration and control of the major marketing functions but less than satisfactory coordination and cooperation

  ____ 1

- Yes. The major marketing functions are effectively integrated with all departments

  ____ 2

This survey was very effective in setting out some key areas. He moved quickly through the next few questions but still gave them careful thought before writing down his score for each question.

When the Marketing Effectiveness Survey© started to move into the area of new products, he said out loud, "Great. We do just fine in this business-building area."

He frowned. “But we don’t really seem to be getting any big home runs. Maybe this survey will help us get some.”

Question 7 asked:

7. How well organized is the new product development process?

- The system is ill-defined and poorly handled.
  ____0
- The system formally exists but lacks sophistication.

  ____1
- The system is well-structured and professionally staffed
  ____2

The scores were not looking good, but Adam gamely went on answering the questions truthfully.

“Peter was right when he said this would help bring some perspective to where CONE Inc. is right now,” he thought. “It might help us to see the key areas we need to focus on to move to that next level of business success." His tea had grown cold.

The next area of the survey was about finance, and Adam was confident they would score well. But as he read the question and noted the trend of the scores, he was not so sure. After all, this was about how marketing was linked to finance. This was a very different perspective than they had taken before.

11. How well does management know the sales potential and profitability of different market segments?

They didn't really examine market segments, which Adam found a little odd. There was a lot more to this area of marketing than he had thought.

He was starting to see how effective the survey tool was. It not only showed what they did well, but it also showed areas needing improvement.

At the end of the survey, he realized the company had scored just 7 out of 30. This apparently meant they were poor at marketing. Now he really needed to understand what marketing was and what value it would bring to his company.

He was eager for Friday to come so he could discuss this more with Peter. To score so low on something he felt they were doing fine on disturbed him.

But first he wanted to see how Sarah had scored her Marketing Effectiveness Survey. © (1) The total scores he noted were interesting for the survey but equally important were the individual question ratings. How had Sarah done?

The next morning, he got his answer. Sarah walked into his office, waving the survey in the air, and said, "Well, I'm not a numbers person all the time. I did some serious thinking for that survey last night and, wow, I scored us only 8 out of 30. Adam, we really need to look at this marketing thing and try to understand what it is and how it can work for us."

"Absolutely right Sarah!" Adam said with spirit. "Let's review our scores and see how we rated the various questions. Then we'll be prepared for our review with Peter."

They spent the next half-hour looking through their respective surveys, seeing where they had scored the same and where they had answered differently.

It was clear they were doing a good job with sales, but they were weak when it came to research support.

They did not seem to know much about the competition.

Sarah scored the product development area lower than Adam. It was clear they needed to get a better perspective on this business technique of marketing.

They summarized what they had learned and ended the meeting with the shared hope that at the next meeting with the three of them, they could start to build on what they had learned. How could they use marketing for business growth?

4

Friday afternoon, Sarah and Peter were waiting when Adam walked into his office a few minutes late, having run over at his previous meeting. "Sorry, I'm late. I hope you have everything you need, Peter?"

Peter smiled, "Yes, thank you. A warm Coca-Cola, no ice, is just what I need now in the afternoon." Sarah had her usual oversized coffee mug, and Adam grabbed a hot tea before joining them at the table.

"Well, Peter, here are our surveys and our results. We scored 7 and 8. Using the summary at the end of the evaluation tool, we figured out the areas we're strong in and the things we're weak in."

Peter said, "What do you think you need to do now?"

Adam said, "Well, I really want to know more about marketing. But obviously, I want to know what it can do for the company before I spend a lot of time working on it."

"Let's start there then," Peter replied "Marketing is one of those things I thought I was doing a lot when I was working in sales. Then, when I started working in the marketing area, I began to understand what marketing was all about. It became clear that it's not the same as selling. It's a group of business techniques and tools to create increased revenues and profits. Now, I know that sounds like a description of every other thing we're supposed to do in business, but it really is the goal of marketing to accelerate the growth of your business."

"For example, when we were looking to expand our Canadian boxed chocolate business, we would have gone to the United States as our expansion market. However, using marketing surveys and analysis, we learned that chocolate consumption is declining in the U.S. but is growing in the Asian markets. So, we focused on the Asian market first. The impact of using marketing tools on the sales revenue was significant, and we were glad we'd chosen to enter a market with stronger options. This helped to fund our entry later into the larger market of the United States."

"When I worked with the not-for-profit company, we used marketing tools to refine and upgrade our logo graphics on brochures, tradeshow booths, and computer presentations."

"Let's spend time today just thinking about why we need marketing or a different type of marketing at CONE Inc. You say the number of products in your company has grown?"

Adam replied, "Absolutely. What the company started with eight years ago completely differs from what we have now. We still have the first products and sell a few of them, but we've created a lot of other products and even bought a couple of products. Also, we've added services to the business mix."

"Alright. Tell me, what do you know about your competition?" asked Peter. "Oh, we know a lot about them," said Adam, on solid ground now. "We go to trade shows and pick up their literature, sales kits, premiums, and promotional materials."

Peter nodded. "What about the pricing area, Sarah?"

Sarah said, "We get hold of their price lists and study them. Then, we put together key business graphs and charts. I'd say the salespeople know what is happening with their competition."

Peter asked, "I would like to know who manages the various products or product lines?"

Adam replied, "We all do. Sales give us good input, and R&D comes up with stuff. We have management meetings where we all get into the act and provide some items and direction. Sometimes manufacturing seems a little confused and says there are too many people telling them what to do, but they work hard and always come up with the answers in the end."

Peter again asked, "How often do you talk to your customers?"

"Good question," said Adam, "We don't spend a lot of time talking to our customers about our products or services. We sell to our customers. We know what they really need, and we get in there and sell them what we make."

"OK, that's a start," Peter said. "I'm beginning to get a clearer picture of the current situation. How do you set your CONE Inc. marketing budget or budgets?" asked Peter.

"Well, the marketing budget is really whatever the guys need. If the sales guys say we need trade shows, then it's trade shows. If they say we need more brochures or updated brochures, we go off and have them printed. We do whatever we need to keep the business rolling along."

Next, Peter asked, "So, do you do strategic planning or business planning?"

"Oh yes," Sarah answered. "Every year, we go off-site from the office and spend two days identifying issues, opportunities, and challenges. We write them all down, and our people get all sorts of tasks out of it. We do have strategic planning."

"We even had a consultant come in and help us set up how to do it. One of the key things we learned was, 'Although strategic planning may seem a sterile, intellectual, analytical process, it's not …the human element is critically important.' [(2)]"

Peter asked, "How do you manage your products as part of that strategic planning process?"

Adam took that one. "Strategic planning really has to do with the whole business unit; we never look at just individual products or groups of products or services."

"Let me sow a seed here for you to ponder, " Peter pensively said. "Do you think big companies like IBM, General Electric, or Ralston Purina do strategic planning for just the company, or do they look at the company and individual products? We don't need to spend time today discussing this, but think about it for one of the next meetings."

Peter went on, "What I think we really need to get a grip on are the benefits of marketing, so you can see there's a number of things it can do for you and CONE Inc. Let me start off by reviewing what you've just said, but change it from a marketing perspective."

"Adam, one of the things you said was that the company started eight years ago with one product, and now you have a bunch of products and services. From a marketing point of view, we need to do some portfolio management to group similar products."

"This will help us to find out which products we should keep, which ones we should support, and which ones we should cut. We need to have the same technique for the services."

Peter saw the worried look on Sarah's face. "Now, don't get too concerned with some of the phrases I use or the concepts I set out. We'll explore them properly later. Right now, we need to grasp marketing from a broad perspective better. I like to call it the 30,000-foot level look," said Peter, and he grinned. "From this perspective, we can see the entire landscape, but not the ants crawling around."

"You mentioned that you pick up the competition's literature and promotions at trade shows. However, if you had a formal method or process of analyzing competitors' strengths and weaknesses, you could look at each competitor on an equal basis. This would allow you to analyze them from a marketing point of view - all their key products and services and their relative positions in the various markets."

Sarah said, "Don't forget those price lists. We look at those and put together charts and guides for our salespeople to look at, at regional meetings. We really know our pricing."

"But the real thing is not just about pricing," said Peter. "It's a number of things that go together along with pricing to add value to CONE Inc. products. That includes products and packaging, but as I said before, this is the 30,000-foot look before we examine the details and techniques of marketing."

"Customers don't buy on price! Now, let's not get too concerned about that statement," said Peter quickly. "But remember it, and when we get to talking about pricing, you will understand what I mean."

Peter smiled at Adam, "Do you want to top up that tea, or shall we just carry on?"

"No, no, this is getting interesting," replied Adam quickly. I'm interested to hear how you convert what we talked about into marketing language or thoughts."

Peter said, "You talked about R&D coming up with stuff. You need to provide them with some direction, and that's just what marketing can do."

"Marketing identifies customer needs, what the long-term trends are, and it provides R&D with clear development parameters based on that analysis."

"But, and it's a big but," said Adam, "that is exactly the kind of thing that stifles creativity. When the R&D guys are told exactly what to do, that is exactly what they deliver! No more and no less. It cuts down their creativity."

Peter was insistent. "Marketing is about providing parameters, not about stifling creativity, putting blinkers on, or shutting people down so tight they don't know where to go. Providing parameters actually helps people to focus and direct their creative thinking and channel it into real results."

"Some people want to pump their own gas. So, marketing takes that group of people or target audience and thinks of ways to offer them better service. And they devise a speed tag so someone can click it at the pump, get their gas, and leave."

"One last area," noted Peter. "You do strategic planning for the company. Have you ever thought, "We can do this for our products and services, too? Don't answer now. We'll put that in our ideas parking lot and come back to it in future meetings."

"To give you some real insight into this whole area of marketing, we must define the term "marketing", and that's what we are going to do shortly," he finished. "Do you have a sense of why you need marketing now? Or is it still kind of a gray area?"

Sarah nodded thoughtfully. "I'm getting the sense of it, but yes, it's still sort of gray. We need to think of a definition of marketing that we relate to and create a foundation that we can build from for other marketing items."

Adam smiled. She really is more than just a number-cruncher, he thought. Then he said out loud, "You're right. We need to have the definition. I want to spend a little time thinking about it. Perhaps we can meet again in a week and create a definition."

"Great," Peter said. "How about 2:00 p.m. next Wednesday? I've got an afternoon free, and we could spend some time developing the definition."

Both Adam and Sarah checked their phone calendars. "Yes, that works for me," Adam said.

"Me too," Sarah said, tapping the meeting into her phone.

"Before we develop a definition of marketing, I'd like to give you a little homework in preparation for our next meeting," said Peter. Forgive me; I'm in my teacher mode. I want you to think about why marketing is really needed. Once we are clear on that, it will help us create the definition that fits your company and its particular needs."

Adam and Sarah walked out into the fresh air feeling a little better, as if they were beginning to understand. But they were a little concerned that they didn't seem to be making any great progress despite this.

"Do you think this is going a little slow?" Sarah asked Adam. She was worried that finding directions and key items to action seemed to be taking much longer than they'd planned.

Adam surprised her by replying, "Not really. It's taken us eight years to get to this point. It will take more than one or two meetings to sort it out and ensure we go in the right direction."

Adam looked at Sarah and could see she was deep in thought. She needed to see the next step to this project. Maybe some discussion time before the next meeting would keep up the momentum.

"Sarah, let's meet on Tuesday in your office and spend some time putting this together. We'll do our homework, 'Why do we feel we need Marketing at

CONE Inc.?', and round out some key thoughts and points before meeting Peter again." He laughed as she rolled her eyes. "Don't worry, Sarah, there's an answer here somewhere, and we're going to find it." They did a clumsy high-five and got into their cars.

Adam really felt ready for dinner. As he drove out of the parking lot and headed home for supper, he began to think of some of the information they'd already reviewed. He was starting to sense there was more to this marketing area than just trade shows and brochures.

"We've already covered a lot of ground in this new marketing business area. Maybe it is the answer to accelerating our business to the next level. We just tapped on how to do that." The thought started rolling through his head, and he realized he was beginning to look forward to learning more about the tools and techniques of marketing.

Sarah smiled as she followed Adam's car out onto the street. "I'm beginning to understand that this marketing is much more complex than what we see around us. Some tools and techniques can be used to really start the focus strategically. Maybe it'll even accelerate our business? The good news is that we are making progress," she thought. We really are making progress."

5

Adam stood behind his desk, stretched, and picked up his file. He had done some "homework" on the weekend and added a couple of notes on Monday about why he thought marketing was really needed. He was looking forward to meeting with Sarah in the next hour to review where they were at, listen to her thoughts, and get a feeling for it all. He knew he should get opinions from other people in the company, but he wanted to get a better handle on where they were going before he did that.

Sarah was there when he entered the mini-meeting room.

After some initial conversation on how business was going, they began to discuss their thoughts.

"Let's look at our services area," Sarah said. "We used to have just onsite service, now we have a customer services call center, Internet Website Q&A section, and the original onsite."

"Okay. And we'll look at competition," Adam said. "There used to be just two main competitors, now there's a lot more. Although they're not competitive with all of our products and services, thank goodness!"

Adam continued, "We do several brochures, but I got them out and looked at them together, and they don't really fit together. Even our company logo is in many colours."

Sarah had an observation. "When I think about it, we all do a great job in our area. We function very well. Somehow, I think there should be more to the process than just functions. But I'm not sure what."

"I'd like to review our notes and then put them on the flipchart."

After an hour, they reached a mutual agreement and added key points to each other's thoughts.

"I am beginning to see that marketing is much more complicated than I originally thought," Sarah said, with her little frown when deep in thought. "But I am still not sure it can accelerate our business?"

"I think you're absolutely right," Adam said. "But I am beginning to understand why marketing is growing in importance, and I'm looking forward to meeting tomorrow with Peter."

6

The next day was sunny and bright as they drove to the university to meet Peter. They were both beginning to feel better about marketing, and they believed they were getting some real insights into it as a business discipline they needed at CONE Inc.

They knocked, walked into Peter's office, and took their customary chairs around the wooden round table in the corner. The sun shone in, lighting up their spirits and the room. Since their last visit, Peter had added a trio of family pictures to his desk, which gave it a more familiar air.

"Well," Peter said, "did you make a list of why you think marketing is important?"

"Yes!" Sarah and Adam said together, and then they laughed at their enthusiasm. This was getting to be fun!

"Let's review some of those points," continued Peter. "Then we can understand exactly what we need to build on. If you're doing fine with understanding why marketing is needed, we can delve into the various marketing areas."

Adam started by saying, "We would like to go through each of our concepts or ideas and discuss each so we all understand them the same way. Does that make sense, Peter?"

Peter agreed. "I do need to understand where you are so I can help. By having a common understanding, we can set the core marketing elements up and build on that foundation."

"For a start," Adam said, "we realize there are a lot of people doing just functional tasks in the CONE company."

"Everyone is carrying out a function, and while they are somewhat related to the other functions, there is no real thread or overall picture other than what senior management brings to it. We don't all share the overall picture or perspective on the project, so maybe we don't see opportunities to add or create value or even necessarily share business-building ideas. In addition, we are pretty much internally focused rather than looking at the marketplace trends"

"Very good," commented Peter. "You have identified one of the key things. Everybody may be performing very well in their own functional areas. However, the marketing function must be performed overall and must link all those other functions on a day-to-day or project-by-project basis."

"So," Sarah said, "marketing is really a function too, but it's more like a management function. It is an overview linking many business things?"

"That's right," Peter said. "But marketing is a very different function to senior management. Senior management is providing direction for the whole company, right?"

"Right," Adam answered. "That's our job, and it's the executive committee's responsibility."

"Okay," Peter chimed in. "Marketing's responsibility is to understand the marketplace and the individual product or core service needs and functions. So marketing is down a layer from the company's management; it's not just looking where the company as a whole is going but where each product or product group or service is going."

"From a decision-making point of view," Sarah interjected, "What we're finding is that we make a lot of decisions internally and develop things, products or services and then provide them to the customers."

She continued, "We think if we had a marketing orientation, we would look at the customer's needs and provide products or services based on their focus and needs. Or what products or services are needed for the future. Like Intel® working on their computer chip 22 Generation Desktop Processor when they are only selling the computer chip 18 Generation Desktop Processor. They are getting ahead of the marketplace needs."

"In fact," Sarah continued, "Knowing where customers are going is a key thing to understand if we're going to get the right products in the right place."

Peter nodded. "That's right. If you really look at it from an economic point of view, the decision-making by marketing touches not just on profits but on the areas of social responsibility, economics, and several other key macro areas. (3) Marketing concerns the whole customer group, not just one individual customer."

"I can see that," Adam said. "That's one of the key areas for sales to understand. We have a key account sales group that is naturally focused on their specific customers or accounts. But sometimes I think we miss opportunities because nobody says if it's good for these two accounts. How many other accounts are there like that out there?"

"Excellent point," Peter answered. "But we're getting a little too focused again on the company's details instead of looking from 30,000 feet. The question I asked you to consider was 'Why is Marketing growing in importance'?"

Adam sipped his tea and consulted his notes. "Okay. Another thing we noticed is there is a slowing of real growth in the marketplace."

Peter gave an emphatic nod. "That's correct."

"Unless you're in those leading-edge markets," Adam continued, "there seems to be a real slowing of the overall economy. In fact, many forecasters estimate the growth in business volume at 2 to 3%, productivity gains at 2 to 3% and inflation between 2 ½% and 3 %."

Peter agreed, saying, "That's right, we no longer have economics driven on a regional or national basis because of world wars or other factors. Now, we are growth-driven in terms of market needs. But go on, what are some of the other things you noted?" continued Peter.

Sarah jumped in, "One of the things we have noted, especially in accounting, is that technology is changing significantly."

"We also noted it in other parts of the company, from manufacturing to R&D, and technology is changing what our customers want from our products, too."

"Yes," Peter said. "What you're seeing is technology impacting what you manufacture, what you create, and it's impacting your clients' needs. For example, look at this computer. Ten years ago, this university wasn't using computers to teach or provide training. Even videos were only occasionally used in class. Now students don't even have to be here to learn physically. They can use online learning at their own pace and access it from anywhere they choose. What else have you noted?"

"Well," continued Adam, eager to share their other findings. "Deregulation is impacting some of the areas we are looking at for CONE. Certain markets regulated by Governments are being deregulated, creating competition and changing the whole marketplace."

"Another good observation," Peter commented. "Yes, deregulation means we have competition, and competition is one of the things marketing must research and handle."

"That's not to say marketing is the only function in the company that handles or looks at competitors. But it's most definitely one of the elements that people in the marketing function must handle."

Sarah also noted, "Lifestyle changes have created new markets and significantly changed existing markets. Just look at the fitness market, eating habits, and bottled water—vitaminized sparkling bottled water! Incredible, things have really changed."

"Overall, the baby boomers have changed how we look at markets, and their wants and needs are significantly different from those of previous generations. And these newer Generation Z people are much more accepting of change. They accept change readily, and they are comfortable with it."

Peter continued, "The other thing you will note is that in organizations where marketing becomes a specific function, the walls tend to come down between areas.

All functions work together to meet the customer's needs."

Adam jumped in, "Wait a minute! We do that now. We all work toward the customers' needs."

"Yes, I agree," Sarah said, "we are all working towards that customer need."

Peter jumped in. "Let me ask you a question. Do each of the functions really work together, or do each of the functions work for and toward the customer?"

Adam answered, "Well, they, um, they tend to focus on the customer."

"But do they work together?" questioned Peter.

"Hmm, good question." Adam pondered. "Overall, I guess we still work by department, and yes, they are specialized departments. The total effort isn't guided by what the customer wants but by what we think we can give the customer. Uh-oh, I'm seeing a picture forming here!"

"Something we mentioned earlier today," Peter continued, "was competition. If we look back to the 1980s and 1990s, there was much less competition. You may not have had much competition even when your company developed its first product."

"But as CONE Inc. developed, other people came onto the market with similar and competitive products or services, correct?"

"Yes," Adam said, "We seem to be generating more and more competition. Why, it seems that every time we create new products or develop new services, another new and different company we haven't seen before comes at us!"

Sarah joined in at this point, "It's kind of confusing sometimes just keeping track of all the competitors out there."

Peter jumped back in. "Yes, and this is why we look at having a business function that can manage that on a focused basis, product-by-product and service-by-service. It's a lot to manage. You have to understand the competition between controllable and uncontrollable elements. Most of the time, we simply focus on controllable elements."

"So that we're all talking from the same perspective, let me clarify what I mean by controllable and uncontrollable elements. This is an important core concept to understand when thinking about marketing."

"The uncontrollable elements are those that are external. Let me give you a few examples to help set up the concept."

"One example is governments. When there is a change in the government and the new one has different priorities, that means new legislation."

"The weather is another uncontrollable. If you have a snowstorm, then JIT deliveries can be slowed up, shutting down production. A late frost can kill farmers' crops, or a storm can shut down an airport. Another uncontrollable is the social environment. The Baby Boomers wanted to participate in cleaning up the environment. That started the whole recycling industry. We have to look at the whole greening area to see how this element has impacted business."

"One big one we've covered is the competitive environment. One company buys another company. Or a company develops a brand-new product or service, and the entire marketplace changes. For example, transistors, radio tubes, or key fobs versus car keys. Take iPad programs versus Android programs?"

"Now, the controllable elements are internal to the company. They include the product, pricing, promotion, and place or distribution."

"So," Peter quietly continued, leaning back in his chair, "if I were to summarize, I would guess you now agree that marketing is a more important function than you thought, and it seems to be growing in importance as a business technique?"

Adam answered, "Yes, I think you are right. We really understand this marketing thing and what it is supposed to accomplish. Therefore, I don't think we've given it the support it really needed in terms of resources or budget."

"We've got the concept," Peter said. "What we need now is to understand the benefits of marketing, then we can create a definition. Let me do some work, and we'll get together next week to go through what I believe are the key benefits of marketing. Then we can create that all-important marketing definition, especially for CONE Inc."

They established a time for the next meeting, and Adam left.

Sarah turned to Peter and said, "This seems to be taking a long time. Is there any way we can do it faster?"

"Sarah," said Peter, "I really wanted you to get thinking in the right mode. Now that you have generated some basic understanding, we could have several meetings in one week."

Back at his office Adam flipped open his iPad® and accessed his new CONE Integrated Marketing NOW! file. "I want to capture these key concepts so I can review them as we move along," he thought. For his first notes, he entered

At CONE Inc., everyone is carrying out a function. They may only look at the functions immediately before and after their function. Marketing looks at all internal company functions and can unify them with an overall perspective, bringing down the current department or team barriers.

So, a CONE business model currently looks like:

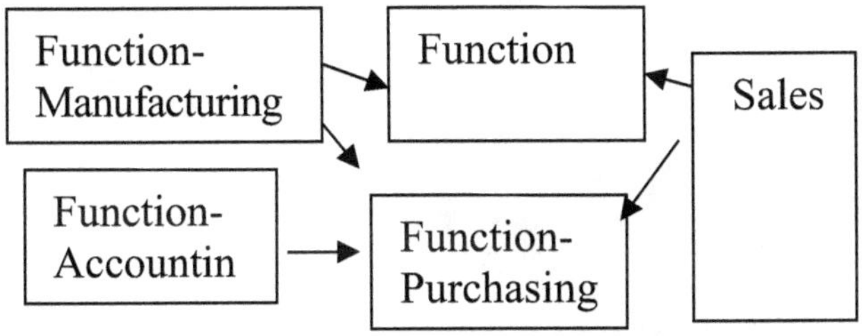

With good marketing, CONE Inc. could look

like this:

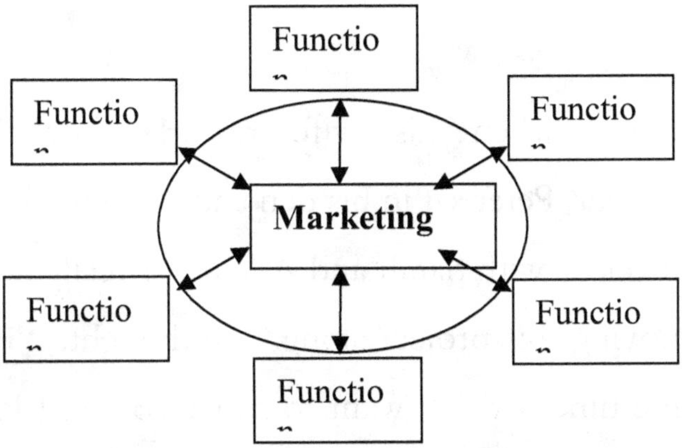

Adam hoped this was a great start to the many notes and ideas to come. He saved the file. He was beginning to see the concept of marketing and growth more visibly now.

7

After dinner, when his wife remarked on his preoccupied air, Peter sat in his den and thought about that last meeting with Sarah and Adam. "I really need to start moving this project along," he thought. "But at the same time, I don't want to move so fast I lose them."

He had compiled several definitions of Marketing and decided to build toward one he had used for several years.

"I don't want to get too academic with this," he thought. "But it is very important to have a clear definition of marketing. The definition will become the springboard for moving the marketing understanding process forward. It must not be so narrow that it limits the use, or so broad that it is not functional.

Looking around his den, his gaze settled first on his books, then his clock, and then his fishing rod. "I need to think of a product and then outline it. Yes, that will work." Thinking back to dinner, he remembered the excellent salad. Salad dressing as a product? No, something more fundamental? What about the tremendous warm bread they had eaten? Yes! Bread. The basic good stuff of life.

If they were to focus on bread from a marketing perspective, they would have to know how many people use bread. And how do they use it? For snacks, for toast, for fish bait, what else? Did they want the bread in rounds, ovals, or rectangles? Did they prefer it sliced or unsliced?

What price would they pay for white, whole wheat, or raisin bread? Would they pay more for bread that was hand-baked, that looked special, or that had key ingredients?

Packaging was another item. How did bread-eaters want it packaged? In a plastic bag, brown paper, cloth?

Distribution was another area. Where did they expect to buy their bread? Would they look for it in specialty shops? How else could one distribute bread?

All the items Peter thought of were about what people wanted and had little to do with what the baker could make or what the baker wanted. If the baker was the greatest animal-shaped bread maker in the world, it didn't matter if nobody wanted alligator-shaped bread.

Peter wrote down a long list of marketing's key benefits to use in the next meeting with Sarah and Adam.

He felt it would be important to provide direction to the exploration of the key benefits of marketing as a business tool.

He finished his tea and leaned back in his high-back brown leather chair. Thinking about all that bread had made him feel full and sleepy. It was time to stop work and watch a classic movie with his wife—to relax, digest, and stop thinking about marketing.

As he switched out the light, he glanced back at the CONE Inc. marketing file that lay on his desk. It was getting thicker after each meeting with Sarah and Adam. He was glad he'd taken time at home to gather his thoughts.

He thought, "Sometimes we just take for granted why we do marketing. It's an interesting exercise to go back to basics and relate it to actual business-building." He enjoyed seeing Adam and Sarah's enthusiasm for the project grow and was looking forward to their next meeting.

8

When they met early the next week, Sarah had already told Adam that she was trying to move the process ahead faster. It would take some time to create the functions at CONE, plus the techniques and tools they needed, and she was eager to move to a level where they could start.

The meeting was at CONE Inc., in one of the mini-conference rooms. A blue-line flip chart stood ready, and Adam had made notes on the whiteboard to start the day's discussion.

Peter started the conversation by saying, "I want you to be sure you fully understand the benefits of marketing products, groups of products, and services. Once we agree on that, we can create a marketing definition for CONE Inc."

"After that we can start breaking out 'How marketing has been successful for various products.' with examples."

"So, let's start with some of the benefits of marketing," he said. "One reason we want to combine products or groups of products to market them is to generate some efficiencies. These will happen in many ways depending on business needs or strategies of the products or services."

"Examples of how efficiencies can come about are using similar advertising creative in several places, such as magazines, posters and trade show materials. Media discounts are available for multiple pages in the same magazine or newspaper."

"Production print runs of catalogues or tradeshow literature for several products can be ganged together to get considerable discounts compared to printing the projects individually. Promotional programs or items we give to clients and potential clients, things like hats, shirts, or desk notepads, can be set up for several products together to get premium discounts."

"By tying together several products we can make the costs lower per product basis. The same as we would if we looked at the per unit cost of raw materials in production."

"Another area is social media. I can tell by your face, Adam, that you're not sure about social media, but let's wait till we get into the marketing mix details and stay at the 10,000-foot level of marketing efficiencies for now. Marketing can create an article that can then be sent to a number of blogs. Tweets can be created from the article. They also could create YouTube videos. All these are an efficient and good use of your marketing budget."

Sarah and Adam nodded and Sarah answered, "Speaking as a numbers person, yes, that makes sense."

"Another major benefit is that marketing can research and understand exactly what the customer's wants and needs are and match that to market trends. For example, if you were to create a product for a leading-edge High-tech industry right now, you would probably not make it an Android-only product. However, if you were to create a product for the Government or a third-world country, an android-based product might be exactly what they want, or at least what they could use, depending on their type of computers. Only research for the broad market can tell you what to do."

"So, another benefit is marketing can define the real wants and needs of customers and the real needs of the marketplace," stated Sarah matter-of-factly.

"This would obviously improve our new product success rate," she continued quietly as if talking to herself. "We would be launching products because there was a real need in the market, not just because it's what we can make."

"Okay," Adam said, "I think I have seen some benefits, but there must be more?"

"Of course," Peter replied. "Let me give you a couple more. Marketing can manage the whole pricing area by looking at not only competition but also your own internal costs and the corporate ROI strategic plan goals. These are all important elements to analyze when setting pricing."

"Is it fair to say that salespeople know what competitors' pricing is for a given product or service?" Peter asked.

"Every one of them," Sarah said, "That's one of the areas we are very proud of at CONE Inc."

"But tell me," Peter continued, "does sales know what the actual internal costs of goods are to create the product or service?"

Sarah frowned. "Well, they don't know the exact production costs or the breakdown, but they do know our final cost and the company markup."

"Correct," said Peter. "However, based on that philosophy, we really need someone who can dig in and tear apart all the product or service costs. We need that if we are to get increased efficiencies or if we want to go in a new product direction. Any number of things can impact the product, affect the revenue, ROI, costs to manufacture and the profit that we make from it. And we need someone who can look at all those areas."

"You might be aware that they have a technique called de-contenting in the car industry. The auto industry has reduced some of the car's content to reduce the price to customers. For a historical example, the 1997 Ford Taurus trimmed $180 off the cost of each car by some things that included using recycled plastic instead of new for splash shields under the wheel wells which saved 45 cents. They borrowed a part from another Ford model to reinforce the sheet metal under the seat for a savings of $1.50 per car. They could only do this by knowing all the parts' costs." (4)

"Why did they do this? Because competitive pricing from offshore cars continues to put pressure on driving car pricing down rather than automatically increasing the list price."

"So, there's another key benefit, having someone or some group focused solely on the individual product or group of products or service. It means that they are looking after the health of that particular product and all the various elements. Just like the mission statement drives the company, these people can take the product and drive that product with certain marketing tools." Peter took a breath. He had covered a lot of material, and a pause to let them think about the concepts.

"I think we are starting to have a good feel for this," Adam said, "but I would still like to set a definition of Marketing."

Peter settled back in his chair. "Normally, I would suggest that you work with your executive committee. But since you two represent it now, we can create a working definition.

"As with any definition, it is something you start with and build from. It must help us understand what marketing is and how it can be a useful business technique. All the people at CONE Inc. must clearly understand this. It really becomes the mission statement for the marketing effort."

Marketing is the management and development of business activities through analysis, making decisions, and executing programs to satisfy present and potential customers and company needs while generating profitable revenues within corporate guidelines." © (5)

"Break this down and we see that we are going to start with analysis. From there we will understand what the customer wants and needs are. Next, we are going to understand what the marketplace is, and we are going to do a number of reviews to understand how to manage and develop the business."

Peter continued to outline the definition. "We are going to make fact-based decisions. This means that we will not only do the analysis, but we will also make decisions and provide suggestions and actionable recommendations. Executing programs means once we have presented our material to management and other departments, we will create programs that will use that information. We are trying to satisfy the customer's needs. That is important."

"I like that definition," Adam commented. "It will add to our company, planning, and overall management process. It will really help to focus the key resource that seems to be the key to several growth factors in any company."

As he took a sip of his tea he added, "I now begin to understand more of where marketing fits in the company and what it is really supposed to do."

Sarah said, "Yes, I begin to see now that it's an overall framework for a marketing process for the whole company."

"One of the other things to note," Peter said, "is that marketing, like any business discipline, has its own terminology and techniques that are the tools to help create the marketing materials and programs."

"As we noted in the definition," he continued, "Marketing works to execute programs or make them happen. To do this marketing people work with functional groups inside the company and with outside suppliers or partners to find ways to meet customer needs and expectations and develop products that can exceed their needs and expectations. That is all part of what they are going to do."

"Great! Well that's another building block," Adam said, "in this overall process."

"Just a quick question before we go." Sarah turned to Peter again, "Does this mean that we aim to satisfy all the customers' needs all of the time?"

"Good question," answered Peter, "The short answer is no! But when the firm focuses its efforts on satisfying certain customer needs, it creates a larger business opportunity than if it focuses just on what the business can produce. It creates a better selling opportunity, a better opportunity for repeat sales, and a better opportunity to keep people sold. That's the better opportunity for more satisfied customers."

"Before we leave these topics, I think we should identify some key companies where marketing has been extremely successful in driving it forward."

"Intel® has used marketing to establish a presence and leadership positioning for a product that few people ever see but many people know about. That's the computer chip. They have used all the marketing mix elements (Price, Place, Promotion, and Product) to support Intel®."

"In fact, Intel® used many of the marketing tools that the majority of their competitors hadn't thought about until Intel® did it first. As a result, they have a huge share of the market, more than 90% in the U.S. overall in 1998. Not surprisingly, they ran into some government correction and now hold their U.S. share to around 75%. But still, that is an enormous share of a large market."

"Southwest® Airlines is another marketing classic," Peter continued, "started with strategic planning, used promotion and pricing heavily to establish themselves. They occupy a unique position in the air travel marketplace segment."

"Importantly, they continue to follow their founding strategy. For example, on the Baltimore/Washington International to Providence route, they have picked up 74% of all passengers, with U.S. Airways getting the rest. They did this by having one-way fares of $38 to $62 compared to competitors' one-way fares at $138 to $ 189 (in earlier 1998)," noted Peter.

"Recently, they lost their way. They forgot what their founding business strategy was, and rather than reduce costs, they decided not to invest in capital spending. Marketing had only a promotional focus, and management looked only at dollars. The big snowstorm of December 2022 caught them off guard. Hundreds of flights were cancelled. The planes sat on the ground with a crew, but the technology to route them and allow take-off was overwhelmed and shut down. Subsequently, the airline shut down."

"Now, I know it's not your area of business, but online e-commerce has some great marketing lessons. One success story is Old World Kitchens' commerce processes, which focused on what they do best: hand-making their products. As they grew, they learned some valuable marketing lessons: Owning a store on Shopify lets you collect customer emails and market your business by communicating directly to your loyal customers to ensure repeat business. Many other marketing platforms don't allow collecting emails or partnering with complementary brands. They gained efficiencies through marketing by selecting the right platform for e-commerce business. Marketing needs to focus its efforts on increasing sales revenue and profitability."

"Great stuff," Adam said. "The more I think about it, the more I can see that highly successful companies are ones that have used marketing very effectively. Sarah, this is definitely something we have to keep looking at for CONE!"

"I think what we have to do," Peter added, "is look at how marketing has been successful for products and services. If we could do that later this week, that would give you more parts of the overall marketing puzzle, in terms of understanding the whole thing. It will fuel the ideas of how to make marketing effective at CONE Inc."

Adam went back to his office, eager to get these new thoughts and ideas about marketing into his notes. Sitting in his office chair, he began to think of how much new stuff he was learning through this key project.

He gazed out the window and his mind started to think of all the impact marketing must have had on the business world. "I've got to admit, it's a much bigger business discipline than I had realized. Alright, let's confirm that definition."

Adam opened the rapidly growing CONE Integrated Marketing file on his iPad and entered the definition of marketing that had been on the flip chart.

Marketing is the management and development of business activities through analysis, making decisions, and executing programs to satisfy present and potential customers and company needs while generating profitable revenues within corporate guidelines." © (5)

Next, he listed some of the benefits.

To pull products or groups of products together and market them in such a way as to generate some efficiencies.

- Marketing can define what the real customer wants and needs are, and what the marketplace can provide or is providing.

- Marketing can manage the whole pricing area by looking at the competition, internal costs, and customer pricing expectations.
- We need someone or some group that is focused solely on the individual product or group of like products.
- Communicating directly with your loyal customers can help drive repeat sales.
- Highly successful companies have used marketing very effectively.
- Highly successful companies continue to use marketing every day.

Yes, there were definitely key management items here to accelerate the CONE Inc. company to the next level!

9

Three days later, they met again at the CONE Inc. offices. This time, they were in a conference room with several flip charts and a whiteboard that could print pages so they could capture all the ideas. Peter had been given his own security pass, and he felt like one of the CONE team members.

"It's interesting," Peter began, "as I walked up here, I saw hundreds of pine cones lying on the ground. Is there anything to do with why your company is called CONE Inc.?"

Adam laughed, "You've got it. It was one of the factors that helped us choose a name when we started up in this location."

They gathered around a table, each with their beverage of choice, Adam with his tea, Sarah with her coffee and Peter his warm Coca-Cola.

They spent a few minutes catching up on the lighter side of life. They talked about their plans for the weekend and the chances of Peter catching any fish.

They were relaxed with each other now, but with a certain amount of excitement between Sarah and Adam because they were beginning to understand more about this marketing discipline. They were looking forward to discussing those elements Peter called the Marketing Mix.

They understood the Marketing Mix was made up of four basic parts or elements: Product, Price, Place, and

Promotion. They wanted to know how marketing looked at those elements now and how they could use them to accelerate marketing growth.

Peter began, "Adam, can you tell me what a product is and what it is made of?"

"Certainly," Adam answered, "It's, er, you know, it's, um, it's got ridges and ruffles and colours and a price tag, and Big C service behind it and . . ."

"Wait a minute," interrupted Peter, "without being specific, if you summarized all those things, what are they?"

Adam spread his hands, "Of course. Features and benefits."

"Exactly," said Peter. "A product is composed of features and benefits that, when delivered to the customer, meet a set of their needs or wants. [© (6)] The other thing to remember is that a product's features are both tangible and intangible."

"An intangible feature," said Sarah, "what do you mean?"

Peter continued. "Tangible is things that I can touch, feel, see, smell, or taste. Intangible are other things that come with the product. For example, I'm sitting here drinking Coca-Cola Classic®. Coca-Cola Classic® comes with an intangible feeling that is created by the brand name, all the advertising, and all the history behind it. Maybe it's a mystique, but intangible emotion, feeling, and image is part of this drink."

Adam said, "Help me understand again why marketing is important for products."

Peter went to the easel and drew a bell curve. He turned and said, "This is a model commonly called the Life Cycle. Every product moves through it. Someone has to manage it at each stage of the cycle. They need to understand where each product is at so that they know exactly what to do in terms of strategy and tactics."

"Some products move through it faster than others. Whacky things like pet rocks or Tamagotchis cyber-pets may have moved through it in 90 days. But think of leading-edge products such as the main frame computer, has it gone through its life cycle yet? No. It is still moving through it. Perhaps Coca-Cola® is at the top of the life cycle curve but isn't in decline."

"Looking at video games, some of them have gone through their cycle, but the overall concept of video games is full of life. Newer and better products are continuously entering at the beginning of the bell and moving through the four stages of the life cycle curve."

"Someone has to manage a product's core service and not just on a client-by-client basis. In the long term, this is where marketing can be successful. It pinpoints where the product is on the bell curve, identifies things we should be doing (strategies), and can identify key objectives that must be used to increase the volumes and revenues. Marketing will pull all these elements together. Using the right strategies at the right time creates accelerated growth."

"Referring back to the definition. We said 'analyze'; well, that's one of the things marketing can do. We must analyze products from a customer perspective and a business perspective."

Peter thought for a moment. "Let me give you a classic example. The Ford Edsel was the most researched car ever created by Ford in the early fifties, but it did not work. Why? Probably because it took seven years to move from original research to the market. In the late 1940s, when the car concept was being researched, people were just getting over the war. They wanted the best, and money was not an issue. But by the mid-fifties, when the car reached the market, many customers had begun life in the family mode. They had moved to the suburbs and had children. Now, what they wanted was an economical family car.

Unfortunately, the Edsel was premium priced with low gas mileage and lots of chrome that needed polishing."

"Now take the Ford Mustang®. That design moved from consumer research to the public in fewer years. And it delivered what they wanted, a sporty car with power, but not so much that mom or dad or the kids could not drive it."

"One last car example to show you the need to keep analyzing and moving forward. The car industry was looking at electric cars. However, big car companies were focused on gas engines. A new car company focused just on electric. It is Tesla. They want to help expedite the move to sustainable transport and energy obtained through electric vehicles and solar power. Over 11 years, they filled out their portfolio of cars and SUVs" (8)

"Marketing can also group products together and look at segmenting the market or creating groups of products in the marketplace. Take compact cars or luxury cars, for example," Peter said.

"Wait a minute," Adam said, "Slow down. This is a lot of information. What's this segmenting of products? Does it come before or after product development?"

"If you think about changes in demographics and take a particular product, you have to ask what the needs of those people are. For example, a car. If you're single and in your early 20s, you're usually looking for economy, sportiness, and image - a whole number of things.

"But if you are 35 years old, married with two kids and a mortgage, you need a family vehicle. That's different than when you were 21, still in school, or took your first job."

"To answer your other question, Adam, segmentation starts before product or service development. It is one of the marketing techniques that helps to focus information to identify the customer's real needs."

"One of the other things," Peter added, "is extremely important for marketing to develop the product positioning. It is a key statement for successfully managing any product's marketing."

"Positioning sets out why the customer should buy the product. It's really the mission statement of the product. Just like a mission statement drives the company, the Product Positioning Statement drives the product or product group. We can have a Service Positioning Statement for services as well."

Sarah said, "Wait a minute. It sounds complicated to be developing a whole bunch of positioning statements."

Peter looked at her, took a sip of his Coca-Cola®, and thought about how to answer. "It is complicated, you're right. That is one of the reasons why marketing must take control of it. However, marketing needs a lot of input to develop the positioning statement. People can generate that information internally about the product features and benefits and what it can do, what it can't do."

"Externally, marketing looks at the competition, it can research customers and the sales force to find out what they are looking for and what they will accept. It is one of those tools that can be complicated, but that is extremely important, and it's one of the reasons why marketing must drive it forward."

"Speaking of complicated," Sarah followed up, "You asked us to break down all the things in a product, and I was surprised by the long list I made. When I started looking at a product like a TV, I said, "Well, there's the physical product; there is the service support; there are the features; there is the quality level; there is the warranty; there are the colours; there is the style, there is the name, and there is the price … holy cow there's a lot of different things!"

"That is great," Peter said. "What you are doing is identifying a whole list of elements that has to be managed by someone."

"Now multiply that by the number of products you have, and you will start to see its complexity."

"It can't be managed just by research & development, manufacturing, or senior management. It requires the focus of an individual, a product manager, or a brand champion."

"When we look at the industrial side," Adam remarked, "I guess there are also things such as raw materials, components, maintenance, supplies, repairs, all those elements that go into making up a product or service."

"Exactly," Peter said, "Now you understand why these things called products and services are complex and why they need someone to manage them who has a good picture of both internal and external elements."

"Also, we have to note that industrial or business-to-business products are different from consumer products in that industrial products usually have a driven demand."

"For instance, we need toilet paper in the washrooms at the office, writing paper at the office, or software programs for computers. We can't put it off, and we have to have them. Consumer purchase of products can be impulse-driven, like buying a snack or a magazine when you're purchasing milk at the corner store or gas at the local gas station."

"Nevertheless, price changes in the industrial area may slow down or speed up how products are used. We will talk more about pricing in the next couple of days."

"Yes," Adam said, "that's something we incurred with the Acme mobile item. Many people wanted it, and we made great initial purchases, but the product has a life cycle of about eight years. Since it was only introduced two years ago, we're still working through the cycle of first purchases rather than replacements."

Adam started to gather up his things. "I think that's enough for today. Thanks Peter, next meeting two days from now, right? And we'll talk about distribution."

Back at his office, Sarah asked, "What was your hurry?"

"I want to get my summary notes entered before I forget all of them," Adam said, opening his iPad and beginning to type:

- Marketing Mix is Product, Place, Price, and Promotion
- All these elements are part of how you "do" marketing.
- A product is composed of features and benefits that, when delivered to the customer, meet a set of needs or wants.
- Someone has to manage the product or service life cycle.

- Marketing can group like products using segmentation.
- Positioning is the mission statement of the product.

There was a wide variety of elements in this marketing area. Adam could see that it was complex but logical in how it could be used for business—more importantly, for CONE Inc.'s business.

Closing the file, he turned and looked out the window. He was momentarily blinded by the sun getting low in the sky. "A blinding flash of light," he thought wryly. "That's what we needed, and I'm beginning to believe we've got it."

10

The next meeting with Peter was held early in the morning at the CONE offices. Adam made sure there was plenty of coffee, hot tea, and, although he couldn't understand the appeal, the warm Coca-Cola that Peter favoured. Sarah had brought a variety of breakfast bagels. Learning seemed to make them all hungry. They needed to spend a couple of hours before the workday started on this marketing project, which they believed was becoming critical for the successful future growth of CONE Inc.

Peter started the meeting by saying, "We need to focus on the whole area of distribution, what we call Place in the definition."

He continued with classic example, "If we think of DELL® computers, they originally had no retail outlets and yet have generated billions of dollars in sales. How? Initially by using a channel of distribution called direct sales."

He paused and then said, "Think of a bank. Today, they have fewer customers coming into the bank since they can bank online. Also, other competitors, such as Loblaws, have credit cards."

"That's interesting," Adam said. "But how can marketing help us succeed more in the distribution area?"

Peter looked at them and said, "We have to understand that we need someone to manage the distribution process. We have to know what the ideal places are for a particular product, what the role of the sales force is, and whether middlemen will benefit or not."

"Wait a minute," Sarah interrupted, "What about middlemen?"

"Middlemen," Peter answered, "are distributors, wholesalers, agents, or brokers that handle your products in various areas, not only in America or Canada but also internationally. For example, it may be more effective to use a broker or agent who can get into key accounts with our products and carry it as one of their products rather than setting up an independent CONE Inc. sales force."

"What! Wait a second," Adam exclaimed, "this is going into a lot of theory. How will I know this is really important and marketing should handle it?"

"Well, it goes back to understanding the target audience and competition," said Peter. "We must understand where people will go to get a product or what incentives will get them to go to a certain place. Know if the competition is selling in certain locations. Then we can plan where to get our distribution and get it in the most effective place possible."

"We are trying to be the most efficient and make the best use of our dollars wherever possible, and marketing's challenge is to find where and how to do that and demonstrate it in a planned, fact-based, and controlled sense."

"One of the things marketing must do is decide the characteristics of the distribution channel. In other words, they need to do segmentation to decide if we need middlemen, how else it could be done, and the channel type. For example, the Franklin Mint sells directly to customers, and Belair Insurance or Travelers

Insurance sells straight to people. They do not use Brokers or middlemen."

"What they are really looking for is that breakthrough opportunity to find a better way to eliminate or reduce the costs involved. Earlier in the meeting, I talked about DELL® computers in Austin, Texas. They found they could sell computers directly to consumers at very low prices by advertising in computer magazines and taking orders by phone or mail. They had no retail outlets to fund and manage and no multiple warehouses; thus, they had low overheads."

"DELL® has expanded again by becoming one of the first companies on the Internet to offer people the chance to build and buy direct computers customized to their requirements."

"Again, marketing identified the new consumers' online shopping trend and explored how they could most efficiently distribute their computer products."

"What is the real idea of this channel of distribution or place?" Sarah asked, "I really want to simplify this area."

Peter answered, "Simply put, the best channel or place for the product should achieve the broadest exposure to the target audience in the place they most want to buy the product. For gum, we want to find it everywhere where people stop to purchase any grocery, convenience, or other impulse products. This is why we have seen the expansion in gas stations of grocery products. They provide the opportunity for additional product exposure, in this case gum, to the target audience."

"Because people pump their own gas these days, they walk into the outlet to pay and find they can buy those kinds of things, like candy, magazines or chocolate bars at the register."

"It will also depend on the kind of product you manufacture. If it's a broad product that is needed for convenience, like paper clips or newspapers, broad scale exposure and broad distribution is required."

"For something expensive or with limited appeal, more selected distribution, fewer salespeople, and fewer distributors can satisfy."

"For example, surgical equipment is only sold to surgeons in hospitals or clinics, a very narrow distribution target. Marketing can make those analyses or reviews and develop the strongest possible set of plans to capitalize on the information generated."

"OK," said Sarah quickly. "Now I've got it. Marketing can set up the most financially sound and efficient way to get CONE Inc.'s products and services out to our customers. Great!"

"Distribution can also offset competitive moves," commented Peter.

"Let's go to DELL® once more. Their competitors thought they had found the way around DELL® because DELL® had no retail outlets."

"Yes." Adam nodded, "that was one of their key success criteria."

"But that was only until DELL® did their marketing work and decided to attack their competitors," Peter said.

"There is a group of businesses called Value Added Resellers," Peter continued, "They are large firms like Anderson Consulting or EDS who recommend solutions to company opportunities. They recommend DELL® and sometimes they load the equipment with software the customer needs and supply it to their customers. DELL® picks up the after-market technical support."

"So, distribution and marketing are really key. Now I see marketing's role." Sarah sat back with a sigh. "Any last thoughts, Adam?"

Adams eyebrows knitted, then he sipped from his teacup, and said "Historically we just moved our products to where sales found customers. We had unique products that worked. Now I feel we've probably missed many opportunities by not taking advantage of this marketing area of place or distribution".

Adam opened his iPad. "If I was to sum up this area, I'd say the distribution we have now means the current sales volume times the revenue minus the costs equals our opportunity profits."

"Okay. Marketing can help us identify incremental distribution, create plus volumes and generate profitable business opportunities."

"Additionally, marketing can strengthen the sales opportunity by focusing on real customers. We can segment the market by analyzing the product and the customer's characteristics. This allows us to identify the strongest segments or groups of customers and suggests where to focus the sales force effort. It's a real ROI approach to business."

"Bravo!" Peter applauded. I couldn't have done a better job of it myself. You've identified the real business opportunity of distribution!" Peter was genuinely excited to see how Adam had captured today's discussions' core ideas.

Sarah shared the infectious enthusiasm, and everyone attacked the breakfast bagels with assorted cream cheese and jam.

Sarah had written the equations on a whiteboard. As they munched, they studied the notes and saw a clear pattern.

"Let's remember that marketing terms can have several meanings, as in any business discipline," Peter said.

"When marketing people talk about the four P's, they will talk about Place. We have been talking about distribution, but they are one and the same."

Adam opened his iPad and entered,

"Our CONE Inc. current model looks like this:

Current distribution + sales volume x revenue - costs = profit

---

Then, capturing his new learning, he created a new, stronger model.

The new CONE Marketing approach would look like this:

Current distribution + incremental distribution + sales volume
+ incremental sales volume x revenue - costs
= profit + incremental profits

CD + ID + SV + ISV X R -C = P + IP ™

"Yes," Adam said, sitting back and smiling. "Marketing would help us take advantage of the place elements."

With that thought, they gathered their notes, shook hands, and resumed their regular tasks.

Each had their own thoughts about this marketing discipline and the benefits it could bring to CONE Inc.

11

Adam and Sarah met over the weekend for a casual drink and discussion. They were in Adam's backyard, having decided they could talk more freely there than at Sarah's place, just three doors from Peter's home. Besides, Adam had a pool, and their partners and children had a fine time in it as they talked.

"Thanks for taking time to do business on the weekend," Sarah said. "I don't intend to make a habit of it," Adam replied.

Sarah grimaced. "Right. But we're making great progress understanding this marketing area, and spending half an hour now will speed up our next meeting with Peter," she said.

She looked over to where her husband was playing with their two kids in the pool and, turning to Adam, said, "All right. In the next meeting, we said we would talk about pricing, and you asked me to think about that because it's an area that finance focuses on."

"We must understand, Adam, that pricing covers many different things. We have our physical products, the raw materials, and the manufacturing costs. But looking at external items there are also volume discounts, there are trade or functional areas, there are allowances, and there are price level guarantees, a whole variety of techniques. It is much more complex than simply setting some pricing."

Adam nodded. "Yes, it's much more complicated than just setting the price." He thought for a minute. "Part of the problem is every salesperson working with a customer sets his or her price, and then distributors have their individual pricing parameters. I sometimes wonder how the salespeople come up with the price they offer the customers. It's complex, alright."

After a few more items of discussion and some note-taking, Adam and Sarah joined their families for some noisy, splashy R&R.

12

The next meeting was held in Peter's office at the university. Adam was amused to find Peter, with his shirt sleeves rolled up and tie loosened, looking very different from their first meeting.

"You know Peter," he said. "We have a pretty good handle on this pricing area. Sarah is an expert in terms of finance and we're very familiar with our costing databases, so I've got to say I don't know what marketing can add to pricing."

Peter started with the following comments. "I would like to ask you a couple of questions. Does each salesperson set the price they need to get the contract, or do you have one price they use?"

"Does each distributor or retailer set their price, or do you provide some parameters? And does a customer have the option to buy at more than one price?"

Sarah answered first. "Well, we know what our costs are and we give those guidelines to sales. As to your first question, sales can set a customer-by-customer price."

Adam broke in, "You know, customers can buy some of our products retail through the wholesale channel. They can also buy them directly, and sometimes those prices are different. It's nothing unusual or illegal, but I am beginning to realize some differences."

"Let's set up a pricing definition so we can all talk from the same perspective," Sarah said in her matter-of-fact way.

Peter wrote on the flip chart, 'Pricing is the exchange of monetary revenue for goods and services between a company and a purchaser or end user.' © (9)

"Fine," said Sarah. That is a core definition that will help us all build a common concept."

"I have some more questions," Peter remarked. "What is the competitive level of pricing? What are the competitive allowances and discounts? And who tracks all that?"

Silence hung in the air as Sarah and Adam pondered the questions. It was uncomfortable to realize they didn't really have an answer to these very important questions. They were confident they had done an excellent job of pricing internally, and they did get some feedback on occasional contracts. But no one was in charge of actually gathering information and analyzing it.

Adam took a sip from his China teacup and broke the silence by saying, "You know, we don't really track competitive information or analyze it to any great extent, except on a contract-by-contract basis if the salespeople provide the information."

"Let me ask another question," said Peter, aware of Adam's concern and slight defensiveness. "Do you have a pricing strategy for each product or product line? Do you have pricing strategies for your services at CONE Inc.?"

"Well, no. We price each product or service based on its cost, the profit we want, and the markup we want," Sarah said.

Adam felt a light coming on, "You are right. We are always pricing it based on discounting and sales," he said aloud. "But if we set a pricing strategy, it might be more effective, and we might generate more revenue."

"Exactly," Peter interjected. "A pricing objective seeks to get as much profit from the market as possible. What we have to realize is there are lots of pricing areas and lots of ways of looking at it."

"A pricing objective and strategy will most definitely help us, regardless of where we are geographically, whether it's around the corner or around the globe."

"We also have to think about product life-cycle again, where the product is in the cycle now and how much we can charge. What are we trying to do to move the product out the door? A number of items must be analyzed and decisions taken."

"Let me ask another question," Peter continued. "How many different pricing strategies do you think there are in a basic product pricing strategy bucket?"

Adam answered, "Educated, guess? I'd say four or five basic pricing strategies."

Sarah looked pensive, then said, "Yes, I'd say five, maybe six."

Peter folded his arms and sat back, looking from one to the other. "Ready for this? There are more than 16 different pricing strategies that can be used. And this is one of those times when different strategies overlap." (10)

"Really?" said Adam, surprised. "I don't really get that."

Peter answered, "For example, take airline tickets. There are seasonal discounts, group discounts, pre-booking and timing discounts, corporate discounts, and weekday discounts, just to name a few. So, there are five different strategies for one pricing item, an airline ticket, and there are plenty of other examples."

Adam began to think this whole pricing area is much more complicated than he'd imagined. He felt it needed to be tied together with other business issues. It was obviously an important part of marketing to understand it all.

Peter was still talking enthusiastically, "You could also look at pricing by market segment or channel. All of those options could add additional revenue or volume."

"Pricing by segment looks at how a product is used and who uses it. Marketing then analyzes whether the segment can be priced differently. For example, at one level, you could price a product for the consumer home office segment that buys one or two items at a time. There will be a different price for the same product for the industrial office segment that buys 100 units at a time. For example, the home office product is one box of paper at $29.95, while the industrial office buying 1,000 boxes of the same paper in one order has a price of $22.95 per box."

"Wow," said Sarah, "My eyes are opening to how marketing can help and influence the pricing strategy. I didn't see how it would relate at first. But now I also see how finance can work with marketing, and so can other departments, to help build the information we all need to make a good analysis and eventually gain stronger profits. The key characteristics of a segment can mean more volume and more revenue."

Peter paused and let that thought float before saying, "Let me summarize. If you really think about this whole pricing area, a variety of policies and pricing objectives can be used."

"They can be focused on a profit orientation, a volume orientation, or a following orientation."

"A profit orientation is for products with a short lifecycle, like software. A volume orientation is for products or services that will be used over and over again. Things like cell phone calls or ready-to-eat cereal such as Cheerios. A following orientation is more for commodity products like gas or services such as training."

"It will depend on the market conditions, competitive requirements, flexibility of the customer end, the product life cycle, and a number of other elements like discounts and actual costs. Pricing itself can change significantly and requires a number of analyses, right Sarah!"

Sarah said, "Yes. There are things like break-even analysis, demand analysis, cost analysis, and several other things that we do sometimes but just don't have the time to do at other times."

Sarah quickly continued, "Each of those formulas can impact the overall pricing."

"Sometimes, though, we don't really look at what we are trying to do strategically beyond the formulas. The formulas cover the inside issues. Marketing can help by looking at the outside influences such as competitors, customer expectations, and other items."

"And that," Peter said, "is really the key. We must look beyond these techniques and pull them all together regarding what is best for the product and what we can actually attain from the customer. Then give those parameters to the sales force."

Sarah took a sip of her coffee. "I was just thinking. When Sales asks for a customer discount, if we just used the break-even analysis, we could see what volume was needed to make the discount work for the customer and still be profitable for us."

"It would seem such a simple process," Adam stated, "but obviously, it's much more complex when we start talking and looking at it from a marketing perspective."

Peter laughed. "Very good. You are starting to talk like a marketing person."

"Well, I'm beginning to think like a Marketing person," Adam replied, laughing too. "Does this mean I'll start dressing like one?"

They said goodbye like old friends after setting a date for the next meeting, at which they would talk about the fun area of Promotion. Peter had provided some information about the sixteen pricing strategies.

As Sarah drove him back to the office, Adam was lost in thought as he reviewed what he knew about pricing for the various CONE Inc. products.

He ran through the sixteen pricing strategies Peter had outlined, referring to notes Peter gave them at the end of their meeting. There was skim pricing, where you price a product high when it is introduced to help set the top of the market. This is the strategy most electronic companies follow with products like VCRs, camcorders, cell phones, and the like.

He looked again at the list. There was bundling, where a company links several products or items together. Maybe they could bundle the service contract and the product together? Yes, that was a pricing strategy option to explore. Just look at the computer industry, he thought to himself. When you buy a computer, it is bundled with programs, a warranty, and a service option.

As he read the sixteen strategies, he realized that one person or a group had to be responsible for key pricing elements if they were going to maximize pricing strategies for CONE Inc. products and services.

Back in his office, Adam opened his iPad. He had to get these key thoughts into his reference file. He paused for a moment and looked out the window. It was a sunny day, and the building was illuminated by shafts of light pouring through the pine trees. Adam allowed himself to believe the future could be that bright cautiously. He began to type:

Pricing is the exchange of monetary revenue for goods and services between a company and an end user. © (9

Current Pricing x Volume = revenue

As he typed, he thought back to the sixteen pricing strategies Peter had given him. No wonder they had pricing all over the place. Without someone focused on it, they could be losing revenue, volume, and profit. They need to get a resource to handle it.

There are at least 16 different strategies

Customers + Marketing Pricing x Volume = Revenue + Additional Revenue ©

CU + MP x V = R + AR ©

After every meeting, he felt the same way. Marketing was more complex than he had thought. But looking back through his notes, he saw exciting ideas and ways to generate more volume, revenue, and profits. He could see the next level of marketing for CONE Inc. Marketing needed to be integrated into the company's processes and systems to accelerate marketing growth.

But he really needed to see the whole marketing picture before figuring out how.

13

Sarah drummed her fingers on her desk. She thought that promotions were the area she knew the least about. Advertising and promotions and public relations and social media were a mystery to her. "I don't really understand what we're getting for our money or our time," she said out loud. "I'm not comfortable with all this, it's not black and white, it's not as fact-based as I'm used to.

"Trade shows," she muttered. "We spend the money on them, but what do we really get out of them?" She sat back and looked around the room. She sat forward excitedly. Advertising and promotion were everywhere!

An accounting industry trade magazine was on the corner of her desk. It usually had some excellent articles in it every month. As the sun poured through her window, she felt a glimmer of understanding.

Sarah worked on the month-end trial balance for a while. She paused to sip from her Cone Inc. stainless steel coffee mug, found it empty, and went for a refill. Standing at the machine she noticed the name of the coffee supplier on the coffeepot Parker Brothers.

She laughed. Despite her rate of coffee consumption, she hadn't ever noticed that name before. But it was the same supplier she had recommended to her husband for his office, so she must have noticed!

Then she remembered going into the local grocery store on her way home last night. The end-aisle display had a giant Ralston Purina poster of a happy woman and her dog that caught her eye on the way to the checkout. She had stopped, turned down the aisle, and bought a bag of new Dog Chow with Lamb & Rice ® for her dog Ruby. The poster had actually helped her decide to buy the product.

Then she noticed her CONE Inc. coffee mug—a promotional item. All key account visitors to Cone Inc. were given a boxed Cone Inc. mug when they left! She really had not thought about it before from a marketing perspective. Maybe there really was an ROI to advertising and promotion.

"Okay," she said to no one in particular. "Concentrate, Sarah. Get the month-end P&L data wrapped up and go home!"

14

As they walked toward the meeting room at CONE Inc., Adam nudged Sarah. "This is the fun area. This is where we get to create things, brochures, ads, and trade show exhibits. It's very creative. I like to think I'm creative."

Sarah rolled her eyes and sighed. "Right," she said. "It may be a lot of fun, but I don't really understand its value."

Adam had gathered up several product brochures, advertisements, trade show materials, and sales tools. He had put them in the room, some on the walls, so that when Peter walked in, he would see the great materials they were doing.

Peter entered and looked around the room. He was amazed at the variety of materials and the different ways they had approached things. "This is an excellent set of material, Adam. You and your company are to be congratulated!"

Adam smiled and said, "Peter, can you explain the thinking behind this Communications area, that 30,000-foot view, before we get into talking about the finer details?"

"Certainly," Peter replied. "Let's start with what communications are. Communication is how persuasive messages, externally or internally, about the product or service are delivered to people. We can break this area down into five different major elements."

"We can talk about the Message, the Message Vehicles, Promotions, Public Relations, and Social Media." © (11)

"That's interesting," said Sarah thoughtfully. "I never even looked at breaking it down in that way before."

"Actually, breaking it down," Peter said, "is critical to understanding which are to be developed, when to develop them, and how to use them. The whole area is key to building the business, and it's more complex than many think. That's why we need to understand it."

He continued, "For example, The Message is what is said or shown to customers and potential customers. By message I mean the actual ad or social media post. It is the pictures, diagrams, and copy."

"It is what they have to look at, and it helps them understand what we are trying to do with our product or service. It suggests to them the benefits of product or service"

"The Message Vehicles are the medium or the way we choose to deliver the commercial message. These are things such as monthly magazines, local newspapers, posters at stores and sell sheets that salespeople use in their customer calls."

"Promotions are short-term incentives or stimulation programs. Things like '*Buy this now and get two for one*'. They are set up to generate sales quickly."

"Social media uses many different platforms on the internet. Like LinkedIn or Instagram"

"I like that," Adam interrupted. "Generating sales is important. We should do more promotions, Sarah!"

"Wait, wait, wait," interjected Peter energetically. "Let's understand that we have to do a mix of marketing efforts, not just pick one and run with it."

"All promotions will do is drive short-term business. They don't build long-term business. For example, if your product is always on discount people begin to believe that's the everyday price. Look at the cereal people with those in-pack premiums or on-pack offers. Does always doing promotions really generate long-term volumes? Not really. Think of the last time you paid full price for coffee at the grocery store?"

"Interesting point," said Adam. "I got carried away there. Please continue, Peter."

"Promotions are short-term incentives, and they include things like direct mail, telemarketing, seasonal discounts, volume discounts, coupons, sales contests, trade shows, and a variety of techniques, emails. But remember they are short-term in nature. Accepting that is key to understanding where they fit in the overall mix of communications elements."

"Public Relations is not paid-for communications or third-party endorsements. Press releases, articles in business magazines or consumer magazines, and articles in newspapers can all be examples of public relations."

Peter paused to let that sink in. As he named each example, he wrote it on a whiteboard as a focal point for their discussions.

"The next point I'm going to write down," he continued, "is that a balance of the five elements is needed to create an overall plan that effectively supports the product or service."

He wrote the statement and put a big oval around it. "This is really important. If you are focused on one area of communication only, you are only providing information in one way. Remember, people get their information from a wide variety of sources including magazines and TV, as well as discussion with friends, the print media, internet and lifestyle situations."

"Yes," Adam said, "but that's why we have the sales group, they go one-on-one with our customers."

"And I don't doubt they do it very well," Peter said. "But we have to remember not every customer or user has the opportunity to have one-on-one time with a salesperson. Think of how many people use or touch your products. Can sales talk directly to all of them? Probably not."

"Another key factor to add to the overall equation is that part of the decision someone is going to make about buying a product or service has already been made before they even speak to a salesperson."

"A 1993 study done by the DRG group showed that when corporate buyers made a decision to buy a major item, they picked one or two items they were already aware of to evaluate. (12) Equally important, a survey done in 1992 showed that many buyers bought items they already knew about and had brand equity in their minds. Other more recent studies continue to support these findings." (13)

Social media has a significant impact these days—a study by k. Rauschnabel, M Brem, and T. Ivnes examines the impact of social media on the decision-making process of corporate buyers, and how it can affect their perception of brands and their willingness to purchase from certain suppliers. A great example of accelerated marketing growth using social media. (14)

"Other studies have been done on consumer products and still others on services. They all support the same principles. People will learn about a product or service and then go out to buy."

"We are going to talk about brand equity later on, but just understand the balance or mix is what is critical."

He stopped to let the information sink in. He realized they had been given many ways of thinking about this key area of communications, and he knew it was very important to their understanding of the impact of marketing.

Peter continued, "I would like us to think of an ad that was originally put out, I believe, by McGraw-Hill Publishing, as it was known then, in the early 1950s. It showed a man sitting in a chair with a scowl on his face, and he said something along the lines of 'I don't know who you are, I don't know your company, I don't know what your company products are, I don't know what your company stands for, I don't know your company's service record. Now what is it you want to sell me?"

"People won't buy a product if they have never heard of it. So, what we have to do is figure out a way of helping people understand what it is we have to offer."

"All right," Adam said, "but how do we know when to advertise, and how do we know when to promote or use public relations?"

Peter answered, "Well, it all depends on the marketing plan and the objectives for communications. The plan will help you decide the balance of the communications elements' integration. It will also tell you the kind or style of advertising, message, promotion, public relations, or social media to use."

He continued, "The marketing plan is like the strategic plan for the company. It provides direction for the individual products and services."

"For example, we could be trying to develop a product early in its lifecycle. We are looking for primary demand or trial purchases. We don't need promotion as much as we need pioneer or information advertising."

Sarah joined in, "Why would you need less promotion? I don't understand that."

Peter turned to her and answered, "If I give you $10.00 off something that you know nothing about, like an automatic glue gun or a self-tapping drill bit, there is no real value in the promotion for you."

"So, $10.00 off something you know nothing about and therefore don't know if you'll use it will not tempt you to buy. There is no value perception from which the customer can evaluate the discount. Money off is no big deal if I don't know the item. There's no incentive to take action."

"However, if you have some awareness of the product and have some perceived value, then the promotion can trigger movement or action like purchasing the item."

"So," Peter continued. "You really have to look at the particular target audience in terms of consumer response models. For example, if we use the awareness, interest, evaluation, decision and confirmation (AIEDC) model as the elements of a consumer's thinking process, for each one of those levels we need to do a different kind of advertising."

Sarah stated. "But everybody knows about CONE Inc. and our great products!"

"That's true," Adam added. "Peter, we're one of the pioneers in this industry, and people know a lot about us."

"That may be true," said Peter. "But remember, new people are entering the market all the time, and they might not know anything about CONE Inc. or your products. They're just out of school, they've come from another industry, or they're changing from accounting to sales."

This made Sarah laugh. "A promotion! A move up the corporate ladder!" she exclaimed.

Peter laughed. Then he continued. "There are also new marketplace opportunities where you could expand, and they may not know about CONE Inc. What you really need to do is research."

"This is all part of what marketing people are supposed to do. They gather information about your market and potential markets and evaluate it. Remember when we talked about the product lifecycle in terms of where the product is on the curve? That kind of information impacts advertising, promotion, pricing, and distribution."

"Very interesting. I know this is good learning because I'm getting hungry," Adam grinned. "Tell me some more about public relations."

"You bet," answered Peter. "I think public relations is one of the least understood elements, perhaps because it is the least controllable element. If you think about PR, it is actually third-party endorsement."

Sarah asked, "Can you expand a little on third-party endorsement."

"Certainly," continued Peter. "Third-party endorsement means it is not a paid-for advertisement, so I, as the reader or viewer, don't consciously screen it out, as you might do with an ad. You must have seen headlines in a newspaper and start to read the story before realizing what you are really reading is an editorial that supports a specific product or service."

"If you think about trade magazines, anywhere from 40% to 60% of the material or stories in them is really public relations releases edited to fit the magazine's needs. That focus on a company can create added awareness and interest amongst the core target audience for your products."

"All right," said Adam. "I am beginning to see that we should be doing some public relations. But because we have trade shows, I don't feel we really need to advertise all the time."

"It's a balance, Adam, everything is a balance in marketing," said Peter. "What you really need is a marketing plan. You don't need to necessarily pour lots of money into the plan for PR. But the structured plan will let you see all the elements and know where to invest your marketing budget."

"What is this social media?" Sarah asked.

"A simple definition is: websites and other online means of communication used by large groups of people to share information, generate sales or develop social and professional contacts. Now, Adam, before you jump in, we will spend time separately on social media. It is not just part of your communications options," Peter said.

Adam nodded his agreement but stayed tight-lipped.

"Ask yourself, what do we currently do?"

Adam answered with a frown. "Well, currently, we advertise, do a trade show, do direct mail and telemarketing all in the same month to benefit from the impact of the trade show. Then we do nothing the next month or the month after that. Are we wasting our effort?"

"The idea is to keep the awareness level or the opportunity for awareness open, so whenever a customer looks at the item they have a high level of top-of-mind awareness. The awareness is there so they can move to the next level in the purchase decision model, the level of interest." Peter commented.

"Think about the last time you went into a Wal-Mart® or Home Depot® or a grocery store looking to buy an item that you don't buy very often. What brand did you consider and perhaps buy besides the store brand? Think about it for a second." said Peter.

Sarah remembered going into Wal-Mart® to buy candies for her kids. She had gone straight to a Mars's®

product rather than the generic Cluff candies. She felt she had a handle on the quality of a Mars's® product.

Adam thought about going into the grocery store to buy a cake mix for his son's birthday. He had automatically gone to Betty Crocker® without even looking at the other cake mix brands on the shelf.

Betty Crocker® was the first brand he had remembered. He answered first, saying "Yes. When I think about buying a cake mix, I immediately think of Betty Crocker® because it's the only brand I know."

"I don't know any other brands because I don't buy cake stuff very often," he said. "Obviously, advertising has influenced me because I bought that one and didn't think twice about it."

"Exactly my point," commented Peter. "Now, while those are consumer product options, the same goes for industrial products or services. We go to companies we know because they already have some equity, some value in them, which makes our decisions easier. That makes it hard for competitive salespeople to get in there and gain store or shelf space. Or get on the shortlist for RFPs. Again, if I don't know what your product or service is, I don't know what you stand for. I need to do a lot more evaluation from scratch." He chuckled. "Pardon the baking pun."

"Okay," Adam agreed. "Suppose I have this great ad; how do I know where to put it?"

"There are many different options, and it comes back to your strategy. Where does your target audience see things? What is the most efficient medium to buy?" stated Peter.

"Ah," reflected Sarah, "efficient, that's my kind of word. Cost efficiency even in advertising is important."

"Absolutely," agreed Peter. "Advertising sometimes is called the black hole, and therefore, it must work twice as hard to show its efficiency."

"Question," said Adam. "How can we measure advertising efficiency?"

Peter thought for a moment. "This is an area where you have to be careful. You can spend a lot of money to generate some nice-to-know information. Given the size of CONE Inc. at the moment, researching to know the total effectiveness of your advertising could be difficult. We need to measure product awareness before the ads come out and after the ads come out."

"But tracking it directly to a sale can be costly and time-consuming, and it may not be necessary until you are much bigger and have bigger ad budgets."

"However, direct mail, promotions, and trade shows, a number of things can be evaluated right through to 'what did we close and what sales did we generate.'"

"For example, with direct mail, you could have a coupon or a 1-800 telephone number. Use a different 1-800 number for each coupon. You could track the number of entries with a promotion by coding all the promotional materials with a different code. Then you'd know if the lead comes from a sales brochure or an ad in a magazine. With tradeshows, you could gain qualified leads that translate to sales by tracking the sales force call reports and noting a when a sale is confirmed."

"With social media, we can track a number of metrics such as clicks, followers, depth of clicks on a website, and others. Let's not worry too much about how to measure. Let's just agree it can be done depending on how it fits in the communications plan."

Peter felt it was time to open another warm Coca-Cola® and introduce another concept. He looked around at the advertising and wall-covering material. "These materials," he said, "look reasonably professional, so you had them done at an outside source?"

Adam answered, "Yes, it is one of the things we are proud of. We have an ad agency that we use for our creative, and sometimes, they do the media buying for us."

"Let's look at these two items here," Peter continued, pointing at ads on the wall. "Obviously, an ad in a trade magazine."

"Yes, that was in the leading trade magazine. We got the outside back cover," stated Sarah.

"Great," said Peter, "and this was the brochure used at the trade show?"

Again, Adam answered, "Yes, and it won an award at that trade show!"

"Congratulations! Did you notice they don't look quite the same? There are different typefaces, and therefore different ways you talk about the product."

"Yes," Adam replied a little impatiently. "And what's your point?"

Peter was ready with his answer, "Adam, you need the same look and feel in all your communications. You have two different logos for CONE Inc."

"You want one logo that is used everywhere! And that is what marketing has to do as part of integrating the communication elements. They must ensure a consistent formatted message, with the same look and feel in any medium and media."

"Think of a company like Intel®. They have been very consistent in their advertising, brochures, newspaper inserts, and dealer advertising. Even strategic partners like DELL® use their logo. Think of the public awareness of Intel®. People sing their little four-note tune! Take another company Coca-Cola®. They focus globally on their logo. Their annual report tells us that Coca-Cola® is the second most recognized expression in the world. "Okay" is number one!"

"Now," Peter added quickly, "it doesn't mean that each ad has to be identical or set up cookie-cutter style. Whenever I look at something produced by CONE Inc., I can recognize what it stands for and where it comes from and see that it's about CONE Inc. Also, products have their own individual feel. Your product lines should share the same look. Look at this product line set of brochures that you have here," he said, pointing to the wall again.

"That's our Sierra line," explained Adam.

"You'll notice how it doesn't really look like a line? It looks like several individual products that happen to carry the Sierra logo at the bottom!"

"Hmm, you're right," said Adam. "Each brochure was completed as the product was created. They didn't follow a style, and putting them on the wall really shows the difference."

Sarah laughed and then told the story of how she had gone into the grocery store and seen the poster. The poster reminded her of an ad she had seen in a consumer magazine for the new Purina Dog Chow with Lamb & Rice®. The ad had appealed to her, and the poster had prompted her to buy.

"Exactly," Peter said, "That's leveraging the same creative or advertising in two places. A very cost-effective use of advertising."

Peter looked at them both and saw that they had taken in a lot of information for the day. It was time to summarize. So, he quietly continued, "This whole area of advertising and promotion seems simple. Think about what you need and develop it. But once again, we've seen that it is not that simple!"

"What you really want to ensure is that you have consistency in your message; you have focused on the correct target audience and the product positioning is being clearly communicated in advertising and in promotions. All the materials must have the same look and feel for the product, or family of products, and the company."

"When we look at this whole area of advertising, it should impact the sales. Promotions should generate short-term sales, but it's only one of the elements of the Marketing Mix. The balance of all the elements will generate incremental volume, revenue, and profits."

"One last area to think about for promotion," stated Peter, "is demonstrating a return on the investment of advertising."

"Oh yes!" jumped in Sarah. "Yes! ROI in advertising!"

"To do that, you need to set up database marketing, which captures the target prospect information to focus your media efforts," added Peter. "You should be adding a website address to your advertising and setting up a database for all those warranty cards and really using it."

"For example, Seagram's went to the publishers of several magazines and asked to put selected ads in by subscriber. They set up postal walks and created certain ads for postal walks ABC and different ads for other postal walks DEF all to appear in the same edition of the magazine. This targeting of the message gets you a stronger ROI for your advertising dollar."

Adam sipped his now cold tea and made a face. He looked from Sarah to Peter and said, "I'll say it again. I understand now that this is a more complex area than I thought when we started this. But I'm thinking of implementation now. And I still need help understanding how to manage it easily within the organization. Can you give that some thought, Peter? And at our next meeting, can you help us understand how to manage this process?"

Peter answered, "I would be glad to. I have been involved with several companies, helping them create the system to manage this. For now, we'll call it the Marketing Product Management System. I have helped develop the processes and procedures, together with your people, to make it very effective. Let me put some thoughts together, and we can meet, say next week."

Sarah leaned forward. "Let's meet the day after tomorrow to keep the momentum going. I get the feeling we can see the end of the tunnel here, and I'd like to get there and turn this into action."

"Always the driver," Adam chuckled. Great, alright, let's look at our schedules. I can probably clear late afternoon if that is good for everyone else. Why don't we do it back here? Make this our business marketing room for now so we can leave material here, keep the stuff on the walls, and add any other charts or graphs we create."

"Done!" said Sarah enthusiastically.

"Sounds good to me," added Peter, pleased to see their enthusiasm.

As they walked away from the meeting, they had their thoughts. Peter was feeling good, knowing he was helping to create real value in a good company.

It had been a long session, but it had made Adam realize that communications was key to any company.

He wrote:

In the communications area, there are Messages, Message Vehicles, Promotions, Public Relations, and Social Media.

For effective communications, you need to ensure consistency of message, focus on the right target audience, and clearly communicate the product positioning.

Message + Message Vehicle + Promotion + PR + Social Media

= Effective communication plans ©

M+MV+P+PR+SM=ECP

Effective communications + current sales efforts = +volume ©

Now it was becoming obvious that this area of marketing needed to be managed to be effective. He was definitely looking forward to Peter's thoughts on how to do this.

15

The day of the next meeting was overcast and threatened rain. Adam was glad they were meeting at CONE Inc., and he was first in the Project room. They were now having all their meetings in this room, which held notes and other materials they created on the walls. It was the CAMG—Cone Accelerate Marketing Growth project room!

Peter was going to discuss how to manage marketing within a company. Their previous meetings had all led up to this one, with Peter helping Adam and Sarah understand that key business-building decisions could not be made without the use of specific marketing tools. He had prepared charts to help direct the meeting and the overall discussion.

Adam sat waiting for Sarah and Peter. His concern had grown since the last meeting. He was worried this marketing project could create a great deal of overhead and human resource issues without actually creating any more business value.

Adam had e-mailed his concerns to Peter and asked him to address them frankly at their next meeting. When Peter entered the room with Sarah, Adam nodded and got up to shake hands all around.

Adam stirred his tea, looked up at Peter, and said, "Please help me understand what we should be doing next, what the logical steps are, and what the real value is here for investing in marketing."

Peter was ready and answered, "Understand, Adam, that there is a very real value, which I will call Marketing Equity. Let's define marketing equity so that we understand what it is and how to value it for your products."

Sarah liked the concept and voiced her thoughts: "Yes, I really need to put some parameters around what the value is of this marketing and its management."

Peter stood beside the flipchart. "Let's start with the concept that we need a central group to manage the whole marketing effort. They're usually called Product Managers or Brand Managers. Product management responsibility falls into several key areas. Overall, product managers become the intelligence centers for the products or services

This is how they do it: (15)

1. By understanding customer needs through a number of strategic steps.
2. By analyzing the product or service on an ongoing basis to confirm progress against specific objectives and strategies.

3. By identifying alternative courses of action required to maximize programs and the product itself.

4. By providing clear, concise internal and external communication to help those resources understand how they can improve the product.

5. By increasing the product's value to customers by successfully using all elements of the marketing mix."

Sarah said, "Okay, now I understand what these product managers do, but what do they actually create beyond some physical things in the marketing mix we discussed, such as pricing, advertising, or social media blogs?" I need to understand their value as well as their cost."

Peter answered her, "I would like to give you another definition before we get into the definition of a product manager. We need to know what Marketing Equity is in terms of definition to build a complete perspective."

"We will define marketing equity as the total value that management can generate for a product or service by managing customer needs and expectations using marketing tools, techniques, and practices." © (16)

"The total value of a product is not just the price paid for it. Take the example of Sunkist®. In 1993, they licensed the Sunkist® name in the United States for $10.3 million. (18) The name appeared on fruit juice, candy and as an ingredient in various items. People believed there was added value in using the Sunkist® name. That was the marketing equity value manufacturers saw in licensing just that name. One more example would be Coca-Cola, which had a global marketing equity of $274.3 billion in 2024. (19)"

"Now, that's a big company, but all companies have marketing equity regardless of their size."

"When large companies are sold, there is a goodwill attached to them, multiples of book rates that don't equal just the physical values of bricks, mortar or resources."

"The same is true for a product. That's what the marketing equity means for a product or service." Peter paused. "The product manager is the key person for managing and accelerating that marketing equity."

"We can take it another step. Product managers' values are assets and liabilities linked to their efforts and the plans they generate. The plans add or subtract from the value provided by a product or service to its users or potential users, its customers or potential customers."

Peter made notes on the flipchart as he spoke. "Measuring value comes in a number of ways. It can be the level of brand awareness that makes selling easier. The sales call cycle might be reduced by one call. That reduces sales costs, gets faster sales, and provides more opportunities for additional calls and sales revenue."

"Brand awareness can impact repeat purchase business that comes in by phone or fax. Orders generated without much effort add sales volume, extra revenue, incremental profits, and overall equity."

"So now we can define what the product manager brings. Now, we need to define what a product manager is in marketing."

"Okay," Adam said, "Let's start with the definition of a product manager. If I can understand that, this might work for me."

"It is really built off the definition of marketing," Peter continued, "because marketing is what product managers do."

"One definition I've found successful is this," Peter said, jotting it down on the flip chart."

"The Product Manager is the Business Champion who drives the product forward through analysis, decision-making, and coordinating programs, using marketing mix elements and tools to satisfy present and potential customer needs while generating volumes, revenues, and profits within corporate guidelines. "© (20)

"I'm beginning to get a picture of this person," Sarah commented, "I'm going to identify some items, and you can tell me if I'm on the right track for what a product manager does."

Peter smiled. The light bulbs were starting to come on, and Adam and Sarah were beginning to drive the marketing development process, exactly as he had hoped. He took a sip of his warm coke, handed Sarah the flipchart pens, and said, "Okay, Sarah, put them up on the old flip chart."

Sarah wrote, 'The product manager is the person in the organization assigned the responsibility of overseeing the various marketing functions concerning a product or service.'

"Yes! Very good," Peter said excitedly.

Adam rose to the occasion and moved to the flip chart, teacup in one hand, pen in the other. "I think it's also, hold on, I'll write it down," he said, and wrote: 'The manager of the marketing mix elements for the product or group of products.'

"Very good," Peter said. "I think also, let's write this down." He rose and began to write below what Adam had just written on the flip chart page.

'It is the person who determines what direction a product should be going and uses the required marketing or business tools to reach those goals.'

"This is good," Adam said. "I'm getting a good picture of this person's role. Are there some elements of successful product management we should look at?"

"Of course," Peter answered. "Product management has been around for a long time. It really started in 1931 at the consumer products company Proctor and Gamble. One of their VPs, Neil McElroy, noticed Camay soap was in the shadow of Ivory Soap, another P&G product. He felt the product was not getting its fair share of resources and sales time and did something about it. P&G started the first really formal marketing approach with product management." (18)

"Equally important though, they wanted to have someone who could take the marketing effort and coordinate it, provide budget commitment, work with sales, and work with the company's internal departments to focus efforts to create marketing equity."

"A study was done by the Boston Consulting Group of leading brands between 1925 and 1985. In 22 different categories they looked at, 19 of the 22 still had the same brand leader after 60 years. (16) The leader dropped in two categories, one to the number two position and one to number five. However, in all cases, all products were still viable contenders in their various markets. Think of the revenue and profits of a product that has been the category leader for 60 years!"

"So, generating marketing equity becomes very important, and the product manager is the person charged with that responsibility."

Having made his point, Peter sat down. Sarah smiled and said, "I think I'm beginning to really get it. It's no good if marketing is attempted by too many different people in the company. Random marketing efforts are not maximizing our marketing equity without the central focus of one person or group with control and authority over it. In fact, we could be making poor decisions that could actually hurt our marketing equity. For example, when our logo is in different colours and fonts, Or pricing is handled just by Sales. It does seem a complex business perspective."

Peter replied, "In his book Managing Brand Equity [(20)], David Acker makes the case that one way brand equity can be hurt is when 'there is no person in the firm who is really charged with protecting the Brand Equity.' Also, when there is no long-term strategy for the brand or product, we are not creating a mental image which will be stimulated in the future. We're not evaluating or analyzing the impact of the elements of the current marketing program."

Sarah asked a key question. "Make it tangible, Peter. How can we really identify this marketing equity element?"

"There are a number of ways it can be done," Peter answered. "One way would be to research a branded versus an unbranded concept. Many people have done this and discovered they could be generating a lot more money. For example, American Motors tested a car called the Renault Premier by showing potential customers an unnamed model of it and asking what they would pay for it."

"Then they showed the car identified by various names. With the Renault Premier name on it, the same car generated a premium price of almost 32% more or $3,000." (22)

"When Chrysler bought American Motors, the car became the Chrysler Eagle Premier and was sold for a price close to the level suggested by that study. This is a specific example of Marketing Equity generating incremental revenue and profits."

Peter continued. "Earlier, we talked about Coca-Cola® and their logo. They believe in the brand 100%. In 1997, the magazine *Financial World* valued the Coca-Cola® brand at $48 billion globally. In 2024, as we learned earlier, it is $274.3 billion."

"Let's consider another example that's not just of dollar value. I think you would agree that the company Apple has a strong presence in the marketplace. Each year, they come out with a new phone, among other new products. When they launch their new phone, people line up in front of the store to buy it the day it is launched. They pay a premium price to be the first ones to get the phone. Think about the extra revenue that's generated quickly from them buying the phone at a premium price as soon as it's launched. You may even think of those as incremental dollars."

"Do you have any products that customers gravitate to as soon as you update them?" Peter asked.

“Now that we've got into this discussion area, Peter, I'm thinking of the WizFin product. Between the government developing new regulations annually and learning how customers use it, we upgrade the software every year. We do it so that in time for the first quarter of the year when we know customers have the budgets to afford new products. You’re right. When I think about it, sales focus solely on the upgraded product for their customers for the first week. Also, though some may get corporate discounts, most people pay a premium price. Wow, I never really thought about that before," Adam said.

Sarah said, "You're right, Adam. Sales really focus on that upgraded product. I see the jump in sales revenue each year for it. I never really thought of it as incremental. But with the premium price, it is a great boost to our overall revenue. A great example, Adam."

"Okay," Adam said, "I can see there is proven value in marketing equity, but I'm still not convinced the product manager has to be there."

"Product management is essential," Peter replied emotionally. "I cannot emphasize this enough. I'm going to repeat, it's absolutely essential! When people have dual roles, they will move towards the one they are the most comfortable with, do you agree?"

"Yes," Sarah answered, "Look at salespeople who love selling, but getting them to do financial reports or their expenses is like pulling teeth!" Everyone laughed.

"That's right," Peter said. "We need someone who can be a marketing champion, as we said in the definition, to drive it forward. To accelerate the growth."

"I know you're right really," Adam added quietly, "We need to have that function focused by a particular individual. But I also need to understand what they can do. I want to absorb what we have talked about so far. I don't know about you, Sarah, but this is a lot of information for me. We've got some very serious decisions to make."

"You're right," Sarah replied, "but I have a good feeling now. I understand what marketing is and why it is important for the company. Now I know the value it can bring to the company."

"Why don't we meet in a couple of days?" Peter asked. "I agree we're getting to the point where you people have to decide if you will introduce marketing into your company and, if so, how you will do it. I have some thoughts we can discuss next time."

The meeting broke up, and they left the CONE AMG meeting room still festooned with ads on the walls and flipcharts full of ideas and information.

Sarah walked Peter to his car. "I can't thank you enough, Peter, for your work. It really helps us understand what we should be doing, and I think it will move the company to the next level."

Peter looked at her, smiled, and said, "Thanks for saying so, Sarah. That is really what marketing can do. Depending on where a company is, it can move it to the next level of business."

Peter continued, "Thank you for letting me work with you on this. It's given me some good insights into how to shape my University 'Entrepreneurs Course' for next semester. I have worked with large corporations my entire career. Working with you has helped me understand there are no big differences in needs between big and small companies. Just different sets of zeros after the sales dollars in the annual reports! It's also made it clear if you do strategic planning, you should be doing product management!"

Back at his office, Adam was making meeting notes in his laptop. He was very glad he had started the file right at the start of their meetings. It would form the basis for the next step of implementing the business case for a marketing process.

In the quiet of his office, he entered his thoughts.

Marketing Equity = Total Value of a Product or Service

(ME=TVP) ©

Marketing Equity must be built and protected

Marketing Product Managers = Product Champions who build and protect Marketing Equity. ©

Well, that was very interesting, he thought. Now it was starting to take form and what they had to do!

16

It was a lovely sunny day as Adam and Sarah drove to Peter's office at the University. As Sarah looked at Adam, she noted his eyebrows knitted together, and he was unusually silent on the drive.

"What's the matter? You seem either deep in thought or concerned?" Sarah said.

"I'm just not sure why we spend time on social media. We don't really need to look at it as a marketing item. In fact, I'm not really sure it's a business item at all?" Adam replied.

"Let's just see what Peter comes up with. He has surprised me in the past with some of his insights about marketing," Sarah said.

They walked into Peter's office and noticed he had a hot tea service set up on the table. They all greeted each other with customary handshakes and good-day comments. Since he told them it was steeped, they poured themselves a cup, added milk, sat back, and waited for him to speak.

Peter started the meeting by saying, "I sense that you don't really think you need social media. Is that right?"

"You're right. I don't really see the need for it. I don't use it much, so I'm not sure it's something for our business. Most of our sales are on contract anyway," Adam said.

"I'm not sure I agree with you, Adam. There may be a need, given how things have changed in the marketplace. But I'm not sure, so I'm looking forward to this discussion," Sarah said.

"Let me share this useful definition of *social media* from dictionary.com. Social media consists of websites and other online means of communication that are used by large groups of people to share information, generate sales, or to develop social and professional contacts." Peter said. "What do you think about that?"

"Okay. I agree that it is a form of communication, and many people seem to use things like Facebook and LinkedIn. But I can't really see how that applies to my business?" Adam said.

"Let me ask you a question," Peters said. "Do you believe your product sales and after-sales are built around personal relationships? Do you think sales spend significant time focusing on relationships?"

"Absolutely. Building relationships is one of our core sales values," Sarah said. Adam nodded in agreement.

Peter paused and took a sip of his tea. "When you think about people, especially those under the age of 35, they have grown up with social media. They spend a lot of time each day on social media sites such as Facebook, X, LinkedIn, and YouTube. Does that make sense?"

"I never really thought about it that way," Adam said. "But you're right; I've been spending more time on LinkedIn lately. It provided some interesting insights into business issues and trends. I've also been able to connect with some key customers just as a follow-up from a networking perspective."

"I agree," Sarah said. "I know I'm on a LinkedIn group for accountants, and we often discuss things, especially when the government comes out with new regulations. I never really considered it, Peter, as part of our need for marketing. But I'm beginning to see a better picture of it."

"Let's think about more ways that social media might impact our marketing?" Peter said.

"I wonder," Sarah said. "If we could use it as part of our customer service approach? We could exchange ideas with prospects and customers to help them understand the benefits and features of our products."

"You're absolutely right, Sarah," Peters said. "It becomes a tool that remote teams working from home could use and still appear transparent as part of the company. Anything else come to mind?"

"We could use it to get our message out differently. I know they have things like paid ads, which I've used on Amazon. I know I'd seen ads when some of the industry association websites were on. It's another way we could connect with our audience," Adam said.

"We talked about branding before. Social media could help us connect our brand with customers and help build or even increase brand loyalty. I know brand loyalty is important in your business," Peters said.

"Absolutely. In fact, we have a large loyal group that really helps us retain our customers over time. Repeat orders are the lifeblood of our business and help some of the seasonal downturns," Sarah added.

"So do we all agree that social media is important as part of the marketing mix elements that we need to use today?"

"Yes. I get it now. I hadn't thought about the social networking site or brand loyalty, but they're very important to our business," Adam said.

"The more I study marketing, the more complex it is. But it's important to manage it. Could you explain a little more about social media, Peter?" Sarah asked.

"Social media can be very complex. But let's stay at the 10,000-foot level for today. There really are four types of social media to consider. Its set out by a model called PESO. This stands for paid, earned, shared, and owned media. Each of these will balance your marketing social media program depending on where you end up with your goals and objectives for the program."

"Well, that sounds like a lot. What does each one of those mean, Peter?" Adam asked.

"Let's have a brief look at each one separately. It won't be so confusing once I have covered them in an overview."

Adam had been taking notes in his journal as he often did. Peter waited while he wrote down the PESO model, heading the P for paid media. "Can we start with paid media, please, Peter?"

"Yes. Paid media refers to the exposure you pay for a third-party platform. You pay to promote content. Just like you would buy an ad in a trade magazine."

"So, you're saying we are exchanging money for content, whether it's an ad in a magazine or social media content?" Sarah asked.

"An example is DelTek consulting. They ran an ad with a white paper download. People just clicked on the download button in the ad."

"That is great. We are always looking for ways to get our white papers into clients' and prospects' hands," Sarah said.

"Yes, it looks like it can get overwhelming. But so far, I'm understanding it," Adam said. "Can we talk about earned media next?"

"Certainly. Earned media refers to publicity or exposure gained from methods or materials you haven't paid for. So, think about reviews done by bloggers. It is similar to reviews done in magazines or newspapers, but they're on social media platforms. They can also be mentions by third-party blogs.

"I remember something you said earlier, Peter: it's like having a third-party authority endorsing our product or service," Sarah said.

"Absolutely. It can have some long-term benefits as people searching online can read the information long after it's originally posted. But like any public relations, you can never guarantee a blog mention or what part of your content they will use."

Peter sat back and could see that Adam was still writing and thinking. He gave them time and waited until he stopped and sipped his tea. Sarah also finished writing and waited for Adam to begin the next discussion.

"Let's now talk about shared media," Peter said. "Shared media refers to branded content by a third party. Content creators known for their continued success in social media must constantly create content their target audience likes, can comment on or share. You can reach a whole new set of followers other than those you currently have when you're on social media."

"I think I understand. So, what we're doing is gaining the trust of our customers or potential customers. Also, comments would be like peer comments and again build trust. It would support loyalty for our brands," Adam said.

"It has to be low cost as well," Sarah said.

"Yes, it can be low cost. But you have to ensure your content's quality is high so people use it. The downside is sometimes it can end up with negative responses, just like any form of communication," Peter said.

"Is an example of this the posts that get reposted on X?" Sarah asked.

"Yes, that is a great example," Peter said.

"Let's talk about the last one now: owned media. Owned media refers to the content you produce and post to your selected channels. It's a great place for brands to strategize and execute their communications. Posted content permits your customers, or - as we say in social media – followers, to interact with the content. Sometimes, they share it. Sometimes, they create a dialogue between you and them, discussing elements about your brand or the content. It can be a very rich source of communications."

Adam was rubbing his chin and staring off into space. They could both tell he was thinking about some pros and cons.

"When I think about this, it would appear to be the low-risk area of the model," Sarah said. "Since we control it, we can manage it. It also would be long-term.

We could put content that's important not just today but over time. Content like safety regulations and how they apply to our products."

"Yes, I like this. Maybe we should focus on this one. It's the one we have the most control over. It would be a channel for just our company," Adam said.

"That's not a good idea. For people to really engage in social media, you need to use all of the PESO methods or, at the very least, three of them. If your audience can only find you in one place, it's like an industrial magazine. You don't get the information if you don't have a copy. Remember what you said at the beginning: social media is about networking and allowing information to be networked."

"Peter, after this discussion, I'm beginning to see some of the benefits we have missed from not being on social media. For example, I think it would help increase our audience engagement with their brands," Adam said.

"I think it may increase or reach our current target audience. We might also find a new target audience of potential customers. I like that idea, and I know sales will, too," Sarah said.

"Thank you, Peter. Once again, you've clarified an area I wasn't sure we needed. But as soon as you said to think about the younger managers, customers, and people who have grown up with social media, I understood how important it is," Adam said.

Sarah appeared to be deep in thought. "Adam, this might be a great area to see what our customers discuss. Looking at blogs and topics they feel passionate about. What do you think?"

"Sarah, you're right. The sales team has been discussing a blog and customer comments for some time. I just didn't see the real need to focus on social media. Now I see that it might be a real treasure trove of information," Adam said. "That would be a great benefit. Plus, we could see which blogs or people they are following for our social media efforts."

"Yes, you both are starting to understand that applying social media has to be part of your accelerated market growth strategy," Peter said.

"I agree, Peter. I think Sarah and I need to stop now; this has been a lot of information for today. A lot of new and really valuable information."

They sat back in their chairs. They really enjoyed the journey Peter was taking them on and could see the long-term benefits to their business with accelerated marketing growth strategies.

17

Sarah walked into the CAMG meeting room, where Peter and Adam talked quietly. "It's a great day out there. The sun is just streaming through our pine trees." Adam smiled. "A great day for seeing things clearly. I've got a good feeling, Sarah, like a fuzzy picture, this marketing area is finally coming into focus."

He thought back to his last conversation with Peter about the next steps for this project and to his almost daily talks with Sarah about the importance of the marketing project for the company's future.

It would come up even when they ran into each other at the coffee machine. It was essential to start putting some form around it.

When Sarah was settled, he began. "At the last meeting, we all took a stab at answering the question: What does a product or brand manager do, and how do they operate? Looking at the definition, we know they analyze, make decisions, and coordinate programs."

"I've been thinking," Sarah said, "In our case, it should be a group of individuals responsible for a particular group of products. They have to be given marketing dollars to research and use outside resources to create things like brochures, trade ads, and social media."

"That's good," Peter commented. "You've got a good handle on where this is going. But it's equally important that they analyze ongoing business. Product management isn't always about the future. Analysis has to be done to learn about, understand, and track existing marketplaces and your marketing plan program."

"So," Adam said. "You're saying we need a separate business unit with specific marketing responsibilities and procedures established."

"If I were to summarize some key areas," Peter said, "I would look at the overall planning area. They need to do product reviews and develop marketing plans. They must have specific templates and formats to plan and communicate objectives. They need specific processes documented so they know where they are going."

Sarah put her hand on her chest and pointed to Adam. "They need the support of senior management. It seems to me that to be effective, they will have a lot of responsibility without authority. The support of senior management is imperative if this will work properly."

Adam nodded. "That's right," Peter said, "it's essential!"

Adam turned and said, "If we want to do this right, we must set it up appropriately. Peter, you've been a tremendous help in getting us to where we are today. We understand clearly what marketing is, why it's important to the company, and most importantly, that marketing generates marketing equity in products and services if it's managed appropriately."

"Equity comes in the form of added value, premium pricing, broader distribution, greater volume, increased revenues and ultimately greater profits."

The rest of the meeting involved a detailed discussion of marketing processes and procedures and how these could be implemented at CONE Inc. to accelerate marketing growth with the least disruption.

Adam felt they would need Peter's help to establish the correct criteria for those involved.

He said, "Now that Sarah and I understand this marketing area, we need to get the executive committee to understand and buy into the whole process. Once they really understand and accept the need for this process, we need to establish a formal marketing structure and set up the required training for marketing processes and techniques."

Sarah smiled and remembered Adam's words when he first grasped how powerful marketing could be. "This actually sounds like the business key to moving this company forward, to solid growth, and to becoming more competitive in the long term."

Adam said, "Peter, I want to summarize some additional thoughts Sarah and I have had. Over the past few years, management has looked at corporate planning. We've identified our culture and created a mission statement. We have done strategic planning to direct the whole company. We think that's been a good base for moving the company to its current position. Would you agree?"

Peter answered, "Yes, that is an excellent start."

Adam continued, "Now we have to create some expansion while managing the products and services. This means getting a champion, called the Product Manager, to create that marketing equity."

"It means grouping the brands, doing strategic planning on a brand-by-brand group basis, working out the portfolio matrix tools and various tools and techniques for a key procedure. The strategic programs, techniques, and policies we use will be very important in moving us to the next level of volume, revenue, and ultimately profitability," stated Adam confidently.

Peter said, "I would like to introduce one last concept to tie this together. It is Integrated Marketing. © We must be careful that people don't think of this new direction as something somebody else must do. Because if that happens, marketing does not reach its potential."

Peter moved on. "A solid definition is '**Integrated Marketing which is the ability to move marketing from a department function to a core business competency for all company functions focused by Product Management."** © (23)

"This goes beyond marketing by the product manager. It means everybody in the company understands that marketing is a part of everything done, but product managers focus it," concluded Peter.

It was agreed that Peter would work as a consultant to establish the executive committee's final definition of marketing for CONE Inc. and ensure that the concept and the committee's need for it were properly communicated and understood internally.

Adam said, 'This all started with Sarah and I trying to figure out how to move this company forward to the next level. We knew we were doing many things right, but we couldn't put our finger on what was missing.

But now we're aware of doing things in a marketing way!"

"When we started this journey, I had no idea where it was going to lead us," Sarah said. "As we started to build up information, I was concerned because it seemed very complex. Then I began to realize that, although it is complex, it's manageable. Just like finance, there are a set of parameters, models and templates that can be used to manage it. I really believe it's key to accelerating our success."

Adam moved to the whiteboard and began writing, "If we look around, we can say:

1. CONE INC. has moved from one product to many products. With marketing, we can segment the products and the markets. We need to analyze the product mix regularly to decide which products to keep and which to cut.

2. We have a solid management team that works well together. Marketing can give them fact-based information on customers' needs and direction while helping senior management make fact-based decisions.

3. Sales are working hard and we have seen they really try. Marketing can provide key sales support tools, effective analysis data, and stronger targeted new products.

4. Our products are a mix of different share levels in their various markets and are of really great quality. Marketing can review the different markets and our competition to see how we can accelerate our volume, revenue, and profits.

5. The company's people are motivated, and marketing can build on that. An internal PR campaign about the advantages of the Marketing program would be a great start.

6. Our client list is growing. Marketing can ensure that these are the right clients. Marketing can also identify

new opportunities for clients and ways to expand our products.

7. Our distribution is solid. Marketing can confirm the right channels."

Then he added, "Now we have the concepts and the direction, we can really grow the revenues, volumes, and profits. I have learned that this is the key to the next stage of future growth for CONE Inc. We're going to do things in a marketing way."

Adam was comfortable that he could get the management team involved now that he had a handle on this new business area. He knew they could be tough on new techniques or changes, but he was confident that he and Sarah could help them understand that there was real value in this marketing business.

He had been sharing the CONE Accelerate Marketing Growth file with Sarah and Peter. Now opened his file and made one last note before leaving the meeting.

Marketing is: Current Products + Marketing Core Competency + Product Champions = Accelerate Revenues and Profits. ©

CP + MCC + PC = AR+ AP ©

"And that's what business is all about!" he said with his president's hat on. "Profits with a capital P!"

Closing his iPad, he looked around the room. "We can take those materials off the wall now and return this room to normal." He took a deep breath and let it out forcefully as he stood. "We've done a lot of good work in this room. Thank you both for your insights and hard work on this important business project. It's been an interesting learning experience for me. And I'm very confident we've found the way to grow to the next business level."

He patted the iPad held in his hand. "I've got it all in here," he smiled. "Peter, thank you. You've given me the understanding to make an excellent case to my management team. Now I can tell them loud and clear:

THIS is why we need Marketing now to accelerate marketing growth to increase our revenue, volume and profits!"

Afterward or
Next Steps/ Indicated Actions

Accelerate Marketing Growth© is a comprehensive journey towards discovering the importance of marketing for your business. After completing the journey, you will better understand the need for effective marketing in your company. The next step is to use this awareness to grow your company's volumes, revenues, and profits.

You can take three steps to achieve this. The first step is to analyze your company's current level of marketing effectiveness using the ESIL Marketing Effectiveness survey. It is a free and effective tool that takes only 30 to 45 minutes to complete. The survey is self-scoring and provides you with three areas of action.

The second step is to pull together several surveys from different departments in your company to identify weak areas and drive change.

The third step is to sign up for "Winning Marketing Plans," a comprehensive course designed to help you develop and execute successful marketing strategies for your business. The course covers all the key elements of an effective marketing plan, including SWOT analysis, product positioning, pricing strategy, place strategy, and promotion strategy. By the end of the course, you'll have a fully developed marketing plan to put into action.

There is no obligation to ESIL, only to yourself, your company, and your success.

Start effectively using Accelerate Marketing Growth© for your products and services now with the guidance of marketing strategy mentor Stephen Rayfield.

Stephen Rayfield CAAP
Marketing Strategy Mentor
srayfieldesil@gmail.com

Improve Your Marketing with the ESIL Marketing Effectiveness Questionnaire

Looking to improve your company's marketing? Look no further than the ESIL Marketing Effectiveness Questionnaire©. With just 15 core questions, you can identify where your company currently stands in terms of marketing and integration of the marketing function, and identify areas for improvement.

This questionnaire is not a complete marketing audit, but it can help you in three ways.

1. First, it can identify how you are currently approaching the marketing function.
2. Second, it can review how other departments are integrating with the marketing group.

3. Thirdly, it can identify areas that you can take action on to improve the marketing effort immediately.

Using the ESIL Marketing Effectiveness Questionnaire© is easy. Just set aside between 25 and 45 minutes to review and answer the questions. There are no right or wrong answers, so be honest about what you see or know about the subject matter covered in each question. Answer all the questions, even if you are not sure. And don't forget to add up the score only after you have done the entire survey.

This tool has been effective in providing a number of companies in North America with direction and action steps for accelerate marketing growth©. Take the time and effort to do the questionnaire and you will have some concrete next steps and indicated actions.

Do not wait to improve your company's marketing effectiveness. Use the ESIL Marketing Effectiveness Questionnaire© today and take the first step towards a more successful marketing strategy to accelerate marketing growth.

Email Stephen Rayfield and he will send you a word copy for your use. His email is srayfieldesil@gmail.com and he will be delighted for you to use this tool. Put the subject heading ESIL Marketing Effectiveness Survey so he will know which marketing document to send.

Notes for the curious

1. Pg. 3 C. Davis Fogg, *Team-based Strategic Planning,* AMACOM 1994
2. Pg. 25 R. Stephen Rayfield, *The Marketing Effectiveness* survey, is an ESIL technique to discover the level of Marketing usage at a company. It has been used by hundreds of companies across many industries.
3. Pg. 38 For more information on this topic see Y.H.Furuhashi and E.J.McCarthy, *Social Issues of Marketing in American Economy, Columbus*, Ohio: Grid, 1971, pp 4-6
4. Pg. 55 The Globe and Mail newspaper, August 13,1998
5. Pg. 62 R. Stephen Rayfield, *Definition of Marketing*, ESIL, June 1996. This is a basic definition.
6. Pg. 65 There are many definitions for product this is a simple one to focus the discussion. For more information see *Basic Marketing*, McCarthy, Shapiro, Perrault latest edition Irwin Publishing or any basic Marketing book.

7. Pg. 68 www.tesla.com for history.
8. Pg. 95 R. Stephen Rayfield ESIL *Marketing User Manual* 1996 - 2023. Pricing is key but rarely defined
9. Pg. 107 R. Stephen Rayfield ESIL *Marketing User Manual* 1996 - 2023. A review of the marketing communications mix elements.
10. Pg. 101 K. Bauschnabl M. Brem and T. Ivens, Journal of Business and Economics, 2016
11. Pg. 107 R. Stephen Rayfield ESIL *Marketing User Manual* 1996 - 2023. Pg. 111 International Data Group, *Buying OT in the 90's: The Channels*, Boston 1992 pg. 83.
12. Pg. 111 International Data Group, *Buying OT in the*
13. *90's: The Channels*, Boston 1992 pg. 87.
14. Pg. 120 Coca-Cola's brand equity was calculated to be US$87.6 billion in 2021 (source: Statista).
15. Pg. 131 R. Stephen Rayfield, *Marketing User Manual*, ESIL, May 1995

16. Pg. 132 R. Stephen Rayfield, *Marketing User Manual*, ESIL, May 1995
17. Pg. 132 David A. Acker, *Managing Brand Equity* The Free Press 1991 pg. 8
18. Pg. 134 Stephen Rayfield, *Marketing User Manual*, ESIL, May 1995. Definition of a Product Manager.
19. Pg. 138 David A. Acker, *Managing Brand Equity* The Free Press 1991 pg. 5
20. Pg. 137 David A. Acker, *Managing Brand Equity* The Free Press 1991 pg. 8
21. Pg. 138 David A. Acker, *Managing Brand Equity* The Free Press 1991 pg. 9
22. Pg. 138 B. G. Yovovich, *Adweek's Marketing Week*, August 8, 1988, pp. 18-24
23. Pg. 145 Stephen Rayfield, ESIL, May 1998. Definition of Integrated Marketing.

Transform Your Marketing Strategy with Winning Marketing Plans

Improve your marketing strategy with personalized one-on-one feedback from a marketing expert in a 10-video training program with a marketing plan workbook. Learn how to analyze your market, target your audience, and position your product or service to drive business growth.

Are you tired of struggling to create marketing plans that deliver results for your business? Are you ready to take your marketing efforts to the next level and drive growth for your company? If so, the Winning Marketing Plans course is for you.

Our 10-video training program, led by marketing expert Stephen Rayfield, will guide you through each model and marketing mix element of a successful marketing plan. You'll learn how to conduct a thorough market analysis, identify your target audience, and position your product or service in the market. You'll also gain strategies for differentiating yourself from the competition, creating a solid budget and plan for allocating your marketing resources.

But that's not all - you'll also receive personalized feedback and support throughout the course. You'll have the opportunity to work one-on-one with Stephen in a 90-minute meeting to review your phase 1 marketing plan and receive insights on your phase 2 final plan. With his guidance, you can fine-tune your marketing strategy and create a plan that delivers results.

In addition to the video training and one-on-one support, you'll also receive a marketing plan workbook with detailed instructions on building your own plan and a business book to help sell senior management on the importance of marketing. You'll also receive written review and comments on your SWOT analysis and a written critique and insights on your positioning statement.

By the end of this course, you'll have the skills and confidence to create a winning marketing plan that drives growth for your business. Here are just a few of the key takeaways you can expect:

A deep understanding of the marketing mix and how to apply it to your business

- The ability to conduct a thorough market analysis and identify your target audience
- Strategies for positioning your product or service in the market
- A solid understanding of your competition and how to differentiate yourself
- A well-defined budget and plan for allocating your marketing resources

- The confidence to present and sell your marketing plan to senior management
- The knowledge and skills to continually assess and adjust your marketing plan as needed
- Personalized feedback and guidance from marketing expert Stephen Rayfield

Don't miss this opportunity to learn from a seasoned pro and advance your marketing efforts. Sign up for Winning Marketing Plans today and start growing your business!

Buy Now

Use this email to contact Stephen to get a quote on the course for you and your team.

sravfieldesil@gmail.com

Unlock the Full Potential of Your Marketing Efforts with Our 'Winning Marketing Plans' Course

The "Winning Marketing Plans" is a comprehensive course designed to help you develop and execute successful marketing strategies for your business.

Marketing is a crucial aspect of any business, and a solid marketing plan is essential for long-term success. A well-crafted marketing plan helps guide your investment and resource allocation and sets the direction for your products or services.

This course covers all the key elements of an effective marketing plan, including SWOT analysis, product positioning, pricing strategy, place strategy, and promotion strategy. You'll learn how to develop SMART goals and objectives and how to identify and overcome key issues that may impact your plan.

In addition, we'll delve into the specifics of each aspect of the marketing mix, including product strategy, pricing strategy, place strategy, and promotion strategy.

You'll learn how to construct an effective product positioning statement, manage the pricing section of your marketing plan, and develop an effective place strategy for distribution.

We'll also cover promotion strategy, including the various communication channels available, developing a compelling promotion mix, and managing the promotion's key milestones.

Throughout the course, you'll work on a marketing plan workbook, where you'll have the opportunity to apply what you've learned to your own business. By the end of the course, you'll have a fully developed marketing plan to put into action.

Here are just a few of the key takeaways you can expect from this course:

- A deep understanding of the importance and benefits of a marketing plan

- The skills to develop and execute a successful marketing strategy
- The knowledge to identify and overcome key issues that may impact your plan
- The ability to construct an effective product positioning statement
- The expertise to manage the pricing and place aspects of your marketing plan
- The know-how to develop an effective promotion strategy and promotion mix

Don't miss this opportunity to take your marketing efforts to the next level. Sign up for "Generating Winning Marketing Plans" today and start building a winning marketing plan for your business.

Buy Now

Use this email to contact Stephen to get a quote on the course for you and your team.

srayfieldesil@gmail.com

Get the results you want for your products.

FAQ About the Winning Marketing Plans course

Q: Will this really give me a complete strategic marketing plan?

A: Yes. This is a proven real-world process that has been used for many years in different businesses. It creates a complete, effective marketing plan.

Q: Do I have to know a lot about marketing?

A: No, you don't have to know much about marketing. The WMP process takes you through every step of developing an effective Winning Marketing Plan. It includes models such as SWOT and how to create one. The strategic pyramid helps us understand how to generate useable objectives, strategies, and tactics.

Q: Will I have support once I invest in the Winning Marketing Plan course?

A: Yes! Your SWOT model will receive written feedback and insights on strengthening the analysis.

Your positioning statement will have written feedback on improving the benefit statement. Your Phase One marketing plan will have a 90-minute one-on-one session for review and insights. Your Phase Two marketing plan will have a 90-minute one-on-one session for review and insights.

Q: Will I have instant access to the entire course?

A: Yes. When you invest in the course, all 10 modules are instantly available. This allows you to develop a marketing plan at a pace that fits your needs while maintaining your job.

Q: Will I need any special software or tools to create my marketing plan successfully?

A: You will not need any special software beyond Microsoft Office and Excel, as well as regular Internet access and a computer.

Q: Will I be able to use this process more than once?

A: Yes. You are gaining knowledge and understanding of developing marketing plans that can be used in your career, hobbies, or anywhere marketing needs to be focused.

Buy Now

Use this email to contact Stephen to get a quote on the course for you and your team.

srayfieldesil@gmail.com

Invest In Yourself Through Strategic Planning.

Free Accelerate Marketing Growth Book Order From

Please send free _____ copies(ies) of the "Accelerate Marketing Growth" book. Up to five copies are free. For other quantities, contact us for a quote.

My Company Name:

____

My Name:

____

My Address: ____

____

City:____

Prov./ State: _______________ Postal / ZIP Code __________

My Email: ____

My Telephone ____

My business is (just a few words to describe your business)

____

____

____

Please send requests via email to ESIL at
sravfieldesil@gmail.com
or by mail to,
ESIL Publishing, 638 Buchan Avenue, Oshawa, Ontario, Canada L1R 3A3

ABOUT ESIL

ESIL is a North American firm that aims to develop and increase the marketing skills of key organizational people by creating specific company learning programs and providing individual coaching sessions.

This development can leverage the product or service marketing equity of the people and the products for the shareholders.

ESIL is the Interim Marketing Development Company dedicated to improving your ability to maximize your Marketing Equity by accelerating marketing growth.

We generate **E**xceptional **S**trategies **I**nnovative **L**earning

Based on our marketing business experience, everyday work in the business environment, and our ability to use current best practices and the most successful techniques of world-class companies.

We have chosen the pinecone to represent the ESIL philosophy

Pinecones are always on green trees, regardless of the climate or the weather - showing a positive approach to any issue. The pinecone symbol represents the fresh spirit of Personal learning and individual growth.

www.ingramcontent.com/pod-product-compliance
Lightning Source LLC
Chambersburg PA
CBHW030934220326
41521CB00040B/2311